UNDER STARRY SKIES

WALTER BERG

UNDER STARRY SKIES
Tracing Our Cosmic Heritage

uvshift
2001

First published by uvshift

> Karl Parkinson
> Uvshift - First Floor
> 69 Tottenham Court Road
> London W1T 2HA

Walter Berg's right to be identified as the author of this work has been asserted by him in accordance with the Copyright, Designs and Patents Act 1988

© Walter Berg 2001

All rights reserved. No part of this book may be reproduced or transmitted in any form, electronic or mechanical, including photocopy or any information storage and retrieval system, without permission in writing from the publisher.

ISBN 0-9540211-0-X

Typeset in Palatino 10/11pt
by Scriptmate Editions from the author's disk

Manufacture coordinated in UK by Book-in-Hand Ltd
20 Shepherds Hill, London N6 5AH

Acknowledgements

I would like to acknowledge the contribution made by all of those who have helped in any way with the production of this title. I would particularly like to acknowledge the valued individual contribution of the following:

David Ratledge: for allowing me to use his astro-image 'Moonrise over Rivington' on the cover.

uvshift publications: for giving me the opportunity to share my personal, emotional and heartfelt experiences with you.

Contents

Introduction: Cosmic Association   9

Part One: *Inside the Blue Horizon: Earth & Sky*

Spring	15
Summer	32
Autumn	46
Winter	63

Part Two: *The Blue Horizon: Ancient Cosmic Wheel*

Roots	85
The Signs of the Zodiac	90
Astrology	102
Confirmation	117

Part Three: *My Blue Heaven: Glimpsing The Visible*

How To Observe	125
The Fragile Shroud	128
Binoculars & Telescopes	132

Part Four: *Beyond the Blue Horizon: Are We Alone?*

Life in the Universe	141
Search for Extraterrestrial Intelligence	146
Enigmas	151
Past, Present & Future	155

Part Five: *The Blue Details: Systems and Ciphers*

The Calendar	163
The Solar Family	169
Fun Activities	178
Tables	186

Introduction

Cosmic Association

You cannot construct the future while hiding the past! Our customs, traditions and festivals are intimately linked with ancient landscapes and their connection to the cosmos. Under Starry Skies offers a multi-disciplinary, holistic approach to nature, the universe and you. Becoming acquainted with various aspects of New Age Astronomy will provide an alternative way of looking at the wonders of the night sky and associating the movements of the heavens with events here on Earth.

Our culture is built upon traditions thousands of years old which have become an essential part of our social well-being, their origins connected to the eternal rhythm of the heavens, the patterns, circles and cycles of nature. We are all children of the cosmos and by using all of our senses: mind; body; spirit; heart and intuition our appreciation of our 'cosmic' heritage will be heightened.

Everything It Takes!

We already have everything it takes to enjoy the night sky: our eyes, our mind and our sense of wonder. We do not need to know the names of the stars to marvel at their existence and their power. Anyone can step out into the night and gaze at the blackness studded with sparkling diamonds whose light has been travelling to reach us since before the dawn of humankind.

We do not need a telescope. The telescope was invented less than 400 years ago, almost two millennia after the ancient Greeks deduced much about Earth's true location in the universe merely by careful naked eye observation. The Pythagoreans knew the Earth was round 2200 years ago. Eratosthenes calculated the Earth's size quite accurately by measuring shadows cast by the Sun. Hipparchus found the size and distance of the Moon by noting the diameter of the Earth's shadow cast on it during eclipses. Observing the Moon's phases and positions, and realising it is lit by sunlight, Aristarchus determined the Sun had to be at least eighteen times further away than the Moon and vastly larger than the Earth. This was an extraordinary revelation which led him to believe the Sun to be the true centre of things, with the Earth revolving around it.

Seventeen centuries later, Copernicus concluded the same thing from naked eye observation of the planets' motions. Soon after, Kepler used precision instruments to form the correct physical model of the solar system. Newton estimated the distance to the star Sirius with reasonable accuracy by comparing its brightness with that of the Sun. All these feats and more can be duplicated by anyone today.

The beauty of the heavens and the wonder of being able to look upon incomprehensibly strange and distant sights is humbling, spiritually uplifting and awe inspiring. The night sky is not only a realm of outstanding beauty, it is also a realm which has inspired and continues to inspire poets, artists, philosophers and lovers and to evoke myths, dreams and legends. 2000 years ago a bright star from within this realm guided the Magi towards Bethlehem. 3000 years earlier, the motivation to construct Stonehenge and the Egyptian Pyramids was fuelled by the appreciation of the motions of the heavens. The foundations and building blocks of every civilisation have been fashioned by the patterns, rhythms, circles and cycles of nature and the cosmos.

The phases of the Moon have even been discovered etched on animal bones over 35 000 years old. When the first humans stood erect, dimly aware of their own existence, humanity connected with the stars. Modern science reveals to us the very atoms of which we are made were forged in the interior of giant stars billions of years ago. We are all made from stardust. We are all magic! The night sky not only furnishes humankind with frontier discoveries but also connects everyone with the cosmos spiritually.

Astronomy, when placed in its correct cultural context allows us to gaze intuitively towards the heavens the way our ancestors did thousands of years before us. Interweaving modern cosmology with ancient wisdom leads away from the nihilism threatened by twenty-first century science and brings a sense of identity to everyone. This sense of belonging springs from understanding our cosmic heritage and our mundane ancestral roots. This connection with nature gives us a sense of place in the universe, a sense of who we are, and goes some way to restoring balance and harmony in our busy and often hollow lives.

More Than Measurement

If you have two pennies
The first penny you should spend on flour
To feed your body
The second penny you should spend on a flower
To feed your spirit

Confucius

Astronomy should be more than the science of the stars. Astronomy is intrinsically connected to ideas about ourselves, our purpose and place in the universe. Throughout human history astronomy fuelled myths, beliefs and ideologies. Even today the stars are provoking myths, legends and fables. Techno-paganism based on Megalithic sites such as Stonehenge and Avebury is flourishing. The ancient values of nature-worship associated with paganism are returning in the form of a wider 'pantheistic' environmental awareness. In the twenty-first century, the US continues to use space to reinforce images of the American dream. The Captain of the USS Enterprise tells us 'space is the final frontier'. The political impact of Copernicus and Newton is well established but we have barely begun to question what effect relativity, quantum and chaos had on twentieth century politics and philosophy, and will have, in the twenty-first century.

The belief in astrology in the modern world, is stronger than it ever has been. The significance of astrology to the history of ideas, religion and science needs to be investigated. Until recently most astronomers were also astrologers, including Sir Isaac Newton who wrote more on the subject of 'mysticism' than he ever did on the subject of science. Astrology can be defined as the use of celestial phenomena to interpret and diagnose events on Earth. However, in order to flourish it requires a social context based on a general belief that the movements and changes in the heavens are causally significant for humanity, even without specific rules and procedures necessary for astrological interpretation.

In order to understand Ancient Wisdom and its influence upon our culture we must first get inside the mind of the ancients. New Age Astronomy is an all embracing astronomy and includes cultural astronomy: the use of astronomical knowledge, beliefs and theories to inspire, inform or influence social forms and ideologies, or any aspect of human behaviour. Under Starry Skies will not only inspire, it will forever alter your consciousness in ways you can hardly imagine!

Part One

Inside The Blue Horizon: Earth & Sky

Spring

I wandered lonely as a cloud
That floats on high o'er vales and hills,
When all at once I saw a crowd,
A host, of golden daffodils;

William Wordsworth

The week had been uneventful. I sat in the university library flicking through the pages of a rather esoteric Science Journal. It was early morning around 8.30 am. I remember looking up and through the window across the lawn towards the Chemistry Department when a shiver of excitement ran right the way down my spine. I left my Journal on the reading stand and walked out of the library into golden sunshine. The last drops from a heavy downpour startled my face. I gazed up to see a beautiful, double rainbow arched halfway across the sky and I took a deep breath. Tomorrow would be March 21st, the vernal equinox.

If you live anywhere in the northern temperate zones on Earth there will be a day in March when you sense something different in the air. The smell of rain-drenched soil, the sound of birds and distant running water, the absence of cold air on your face and the feeling you are less cut off from the Earth, the sky and nature. It is the arrival of spring. There are sights in the night sky too which you associate with spring every bit as much as disappearing robins, golden daffodils and brightly coloured tulips. Let us take a tour of some of these celestial attractions and examine the sway each held over our ancestors and the influence each exerts on our lives today.

Vernal means 'spring' and equinox means 'equal night'. On the day of the spring equinox, night and day are of equal length, each lasting exactly twelve hours. Spring arrives when the Earth is tilted so the Sun is directly over the equator. In the northern parts of the world the first day of spring occurs around March 21st, though the date may vary slightly. In the southern parts of the world the seasons are opposite to those of the northern hemisphere and so it is the autumn equinox which occurs around March 21st.

Ancient cultures celebrated spring and associated the season with the return of life to the Earth. Spring's arrival was of more consequence than it is for us today. Winter food shortages ended, crops could be planted and people did not have to worry about staying warm as they had struggled to do during winter. In our modern world, more insulated from the progress of the seasons, we turn up our central heating and visit our local supermarket to buy vegetables and fruit which are available all year round, no matter what the season.

The most important point to understand about all of our festival days is that they imposed themselves on humankind. Our festival days were chosen not to commemorate an historical event or to observe important social institutions. These days existed long before humankind existed, or the dinosaurs, or any life on this planet. Our festival days of which there are eight are as old as the Earth itself. These days are so old because they are part of the Earth's natural rhythm, they are part of nature.

The Earth's axis is tilted slightly to the plane of the solar system and consequently once a year the longest night is accompanied by the shortest day: the winter solstice. Exactly opposite on the wheel of the year, the longest day is accompanied by the shortest night: the summer solstice. Each spring there comes a day when the hours between the Sun rising and the Sun setting are exactly equal to the hours between the Sun setting and the Sun rising: the vernal equinox. At the autumn equinox the hours of darkness and the hours of daylight are also exactly in balance. The importance of these four days lies in the fact they were not invented. Our ancestors simply noted the changing hours of daylight and the changing patterns of the seasons. The ancients were tuned into the rhythms and cycles of the cosmos.

Our pagan ancestors began the springtime season in February which continued until April 30th. May 1st saw the first morning of summer. The vernal equinox represented the spring season's apex, halfway through the journey from Imbolc (Candlemas) and Bealtaine, February 2nd and May 1st respectively. The year is naturally divided into four equinox and solstice days called quarter days. Four other days intersect these quarter days falling at the mid point of each and are called cross quarter days. The cross quarter days were more important than the solstice or equinox quarter days in Celtic culture. Events reach their greatest strength, their moment of peak energy at their midpoint. In observing a human life a person is usually at the apex of health and vitality at a point about halfway through their mortality. It is the same in nature. The cross quarter days were seen as the four 'power points' of the year, a turning of the seasons.

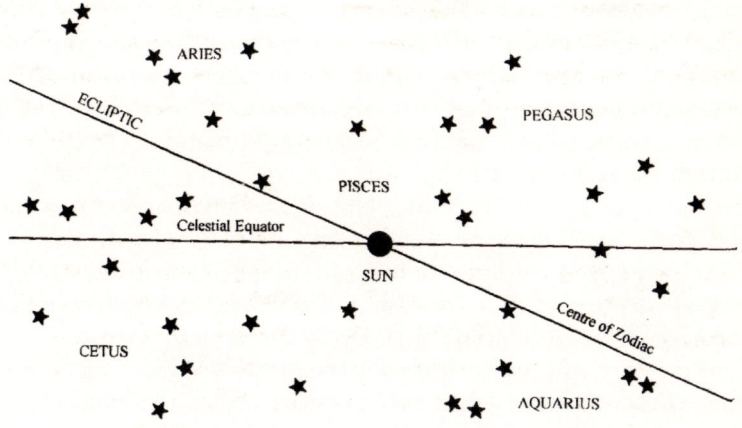

Fig 1 THE VERNAL EQUINOX Around March 21st each year the Sun crosses the celestial equator travelling north along the ecliptic: the spring equinox. This now occurs in the zodiac sign of Pisces and not Aries

Easter

The lunar goddess of dawn and spring, Eoster celebrated her holiday on the first Full Moon after the spring equinox. The Norse Eoster 'season of the growing Sun' occurred throughout April. The word Eoster is derived from the Babylonian Ishtar, the Moon Goddess. The name of the month of March arises from the Roman god Mars and the name April from the Greek goddess Aphrodite, who is identified with the Roman Venus. The Anglo Saxon month of April is dedicated to 'Eoster-monath'. The Christian holiday of Easter whose name is derived from Eoster often falls in April and replaced the lunar pagan festival of the spring deity; fertility and new life. (The name of the female hormone oestrogen is derived from the same lunar source.) Spring festivals were held and bonfires lit thousands of years before the Western branch of the universal Church of Christ arrived. They were lit to celebrate the changing of the seasons and the endless rhythms of nature and the cosmos.

Our cosmic heritage hails from many cultures: the Megalithic peoples who inhabited the British Isles 5000 years ago and the Celtic peoples who arrived in the British Isles from northern

Europe around 2500 years ago. Other cultural influences: Greek, Babylonian were introduced by the Roman invasion and later, Christianity added greatly to our cultural landscape.

Little is known of the Megalithic communities save their enigmatic works which are spread throughout Brittany and the British Isles and which significantly influenced the Celtic peoples. Over a period of two millennia from around 3500 BC to 1600 BC these people erected hundreds of standing stones and constructed dozens of Megalithic sites including New Grange in Ireland, Callanish in the Outer Hebrides, Tinkinswood in Wales and the most famous of all, Stonehenge in England. Many of these sites are considered to be not only temples and models of sacred geometry but precise cylindrical and astronomical 'computers' (solar/lunar), their every dimension precise.

When the Celtic tribes arrived in the British Isles they found only memories of those who had built the stone circles a full millennium before. Not even the Druids, the Celtic priesthood knew the full meaning of the Megalithic stones. However, the Druids acknowledged the legacy of their mysterious predecessors as representing a greater wisdom and the stones became sacred sites and thus were preserved within Celtic, Roman and Christian culture.

Celtic peoples were not skilled in precise astronomical observation, in predicting accurately the movement of the Sun and Moon. Megalithic, Mediterranean and Middle Eastern peoples were. Watching the heavens turning overhead, the Celts thought of the year's progression as a wheel or circle. The circular motif and similar symbols such as the spiral, can be a reminder of the constant movement of the universe, of the potential for growth and development. This Sun wise motion of the wheel with seemingly no beginning nor end signified that as one cycle ended, another began, and the cycles continued in an eternal rhythm.

The Celtic Year Wheel displayed the two main fire festivals: Bealtaine and Samhain, the beginning of summer and the beginning of winter, respectively. Two other fire festivals, also displayed on the Wheel, Imbolc and Lughnasadh were celebrated in February and August. Fire represented the Sun. With the passage of time the Druid priesthood learned the Megalithic stone monuments were associated with astronomical events: the solstices and equinoxes.

The influence of the Romans also gradually led the Celts to include solar events in their festival dates and the Celtic year wheel became divided into eight parts. The new additions were called low days or quarter days, the original Celtic four being called high days or cross quarter days. Megalithic and Roman peoples acknowledged the spring equinox as the beginning of the season as we still do today.

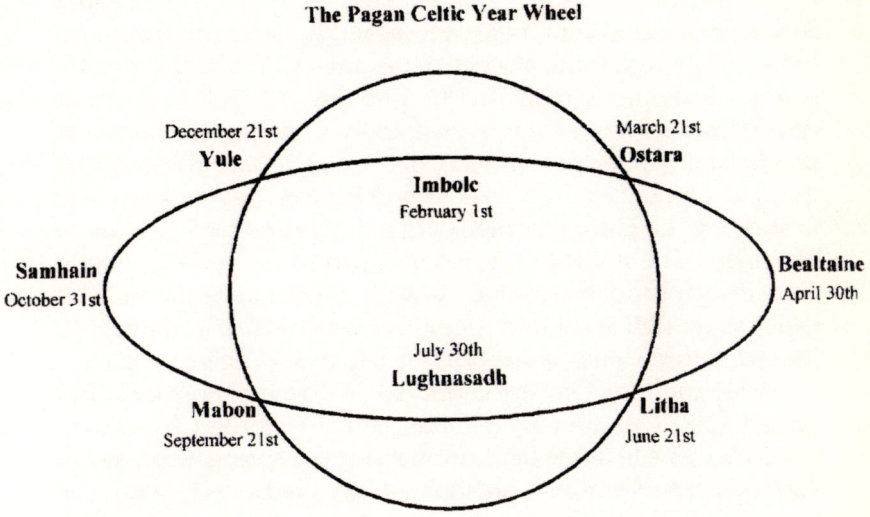

Fig 2 PAGAN CELTIC WHEEL OF THE YEAR The ellipse represents the original pagan Sabbats or high-days. The circle represents the solar year of solstices and equinoxes which in- tersects the ellipse on the quarter days or low-days

The Celts were strongly influenced by lunar cycles and the feminine, intuitive Moon played an important part in their mythology. The Celts used a thirteen lunar zodiac calendar. The lunar influence diminished as the older Celtic traditions were reformed by the Druids, who in turn influenced the Roman religion. Gradually the old pagan landscape was absorbed within the new of Christianity. The Celtic Church did not break with tradition, but continued in essence within the new form. The Christian tradition retained influences from ancient pagan festivals as well as transferring the traits of many mythological figures from deities to saints. Megalithic, pagan and Celtic peoples understood all existence as cyclical in nature. They saw a direct continuity between the material world, the spiritual world and the heavenly world. For them, nature and the cosmos existed on several simultaneous levels: the physical, the spiritual and the symbolic.

The word 'pagan' is derived from the Latin paganus 'countryman' and is synonymous with 'heathen' (of the heath or of the moor). Nature worship, whereby the elements, trees, earth, rivers, seas and sky are perceived as alive, each with their own indwelling spirit, is the essence of paganism. A modified paganism is enjoying a modest but growing revival today. The environmental movement is essentially a 'wider paganism' or pantheism. Modern societies' evils, from Blake's dark satanic mills to Oppenheimer's atomic bomb have polluted and are destroying the Earth, its fragile atmosphere and its finely tuned biosphere. The revival of a wider paganism, especially among Gaia-Principle adherents and New Age environmentalists who feel that enough is enough, signifies a renewed connection with the old nature values of Megalithic, pagan and Celtic peoples.

Easter and May Day are celebrated with even more glitz and razzamatazz than they were thousands of years ago. Every city, town and village in the land commemorates spring. In an age of super-duper electronic technology we reconnect with the patterns, rhythms, circles and cycles of the cosmos each season, as our ancestors did before us. We still see springtime as a season of renewal where green things grow, birds sing, animals re-appear from hibernations, frogs leap, bats twitter and we feel a renewal of energy within ourselves. We begin to wear lighter and brighter coloured clothing to match the environment around us. Spring-cleaning happens at two levels. Physically, we get rid of material things we no longer need or believe to be useful. Spiritually, we discard gloomy winter energy and embrace the newness and life of spring. We even fall in love. The lines from the poem 'Locksley Hall' by Alfred Lord Tennyson remind us: 'In the spring a livelier iris changes on the burnish'd dove; In the spring a young man's fancy lightly turns to thoughts of love'

Sabbath

This period of energy renewal is confirmed at the equinox where light and darkness are in balance, but the light is mastering the darkness. The equinox and solstice are in essence solar festivals (not lunar). The solstice invader (the Sun) first added Yule and

Midsummer to the four great pagan Sabbats and finally the spring and autumnal equinox.

The word 'Sabbat' (Sabbath) derives from Babylon, meaning 'Heart-rest'; originally, the day of rest taken by the Moon when full, neither increasing nor decreasing. On this day, it was said Ishtar the Moon Goddess was menstruating and it would be unlucky or taboo to work, eat cooked food or go on a journey. Incidentally, these prohibitions were placed mainly on women. Originally observed monthly, the taboo was later observed at the Moon's quarters or weekly on the seventh day. Christianity teaches that God rested on the seventh day after the Creation. This displaced the feminine, lunar element. Later came the Christian annexation of the Mithraic 'Sun-day'. Monday, or Moon-day is more appropriately the Sabbath day which is also truer to the feminine spirit. Mithras is the ancient Persian God of Light who became popular in the Roman Empire.

The original four great pagan Sabbats were depicted by a circle divided into four equal parts. The quarter circle motif is an archetypal symbol, later adopted by Jung, representing wholeness and balance. Primordial archetypal images do not arise from personal memory or experience but seemingly from an ancient vast universal store of imagery located deep within the unconscious of humanity. This is why archetypal symbols have been recognised universally throughout history. The pagan solar fire wheel containing four points within a circle joined by a cross occurs in the symbolism of many cultures.

The Celtic cross has been used as a symbol of mystery for thousands of years. The cross associated with the crucifixion of Christ is a Roman cross. The Celtic cross is infused with a great variety of social symbolism: the lucky four leafed clover, the magic circle with its four cardinal candles and even the humble hot cross bun. Wheat cakes were baked in Eoster's honour and though the early church forbade the Celtic fire rites, the Anglo Saxons continued to bake cakes with the Celtic cross scored on the mix. They became known as hot cross buns. My family bake hot cross buns each Easter and we all enjoy eating them!

The Easter rabbit is a symbol of fertility, arising from the (hare) Moon laying eggs for children to eat. The Easter egg represented the world (egg) laid by the feminine Moon goddess and split open by the heat of the masculine Sun god. The hatching out of the world is celebrated each year. The Easter bunny forms a part of these ancient traditions, because of the rabbits' prodigious breeding habits. Today the Easter egg, painted with bright colours to represent the bright sunny colours of spring, is used in Easter egg rolling contests and given as a gift. In the small village of Olney, near to Bedford, a famous Easter egg and spoon race that attracts international media attention takes place each year. Olney is also the village where John Newton composed the hymn Amazing Grace, (Olney Hymns) a favourite of mine which I often sing in the bath: 'Amazing Grace, how sweet the sound. That saved a wretch like me'.

Lent

The old Anglo Saxon word Lenctentide means 'the time of lengthening' and the month of March was called Lencten monath, later becoming Lent. Another seasonal cake associated with Lent was mothering cake or simnel cake, a rich fruitcake. The Lenten fast dictated the simnel cake had to keep until Easter. The cake was boiled in water, baked and finished with icing. Sometimes the crust was of flour and water, coloured with saffron. The earliest Mother's Day celebrations are traced back to the spring celebrations of ancient Greece in honour of Rhea, wife of Cronus and the Mother of the gods and goddesses. In Rome the most significant Mother's Day festival was dedicated to the worship of Cybele, another mother goddess. Ceremonies in her honour began some 2250 years ago.

The Maypole and its dance is a remnant of the old festivities and the May Queen is the universal virgin. They were all part of spring fertility rituals. On May Day, walking the circuit of one's property (beating the bounds) and erecting boundary markers was undertaken. Processions of milkmaids, Morris dancers, feasting, music, drinking, maidens bathing their face in the morning dew of May to retain their youthful looks, all stem from Megalithic and Celtic rituals. There is no reason to doubt that both the celebrations of ancient Celtic festivals and the rituals performed at Megalithic stone circles included dance. Morris dancing has been claimed to be a remnant of a pre Christian Celtic Druid fertility dance. Folklore, indeed Shakespeare (All's Well that Ends Well) makes it clear that the Morris dance was commonly preformed on May Day and had been so from time immemorial.

The dating of modern Easter was undertaken by the Council of Nicaea and calculated at Alexandra, then the principal astronomical centre of the world. In the 4th century AD, Easter was celebrated on the first Sunday after the Full Moon following the vernal equinox (as it is today). Unfortunately, the equinox kept slipping backwards on the calendar one full day every 130 years and by 1500 the vernal equinox fell on March 10th. The problem created an inconsistency between the true astronomical year and the Julian calendar. The predicament was only resolved in 1582 by Pope Gregory XIII who introduced a new and more accurate calendar. The interesting point is Easter is still set by the movement of the Earth, the Megalithic Sun and the Celtic Moon, and the months in which it can occur are named after the planets Mars and Venus.

The Gregorian calendar proclaimed from Rome was adopted immediately in Catholic countries. Protestant countries followed more slowly. Protestant regions in Germany and the northern Netherlands adopted the calendar within decades. The English (and her colonies) retained the Julian Calendar for another 150 years. Moreover, the Gregorian calendar began the New Year on January 1st, while the English began the New Year on March 25th, an older custom. The date February 11th 1672 in England was February 21st 1673 on the Continent.

The early Roman calendar used March 1st as New Years Day. Later the ancient Romans made January 1st the beginning of the year. During the Middle Ages, most European countries used March 25th, a Christian holiday called Annunciation Day, to start the year. The tradition of 'All Fools Day' or April Fools day began in the mid-sixteenth century when France began to celebrate the New Year on January 1st. Communications were slow 400 years ago and many people continued to celebrate New Years Day around April 1st. These misinformed individuals were referred to as 'April Fools' and had tricks played on them.

Spring Time

My dog is called Red. He's a red setter. I know his name isn't very innovative but when we (my family) first saw him we just had to call him Red. Red and I have spent many nights under the stars in all weathers and in all seasons and I can't tell you how much I love being with him. 'Me, Red and the universe' make a great team. I say to Red 'Red, we are a great team', and Red nods his head knowingly. You can be part of a great team too. Step out into the night. Spend a couple of hours walking under a clear sky. Look up at the stars or the Moon or simply enjoy the splendour and magic of evening and dawn twilights. Try and connect with your ancestors who looked at the same sky thousands of years before you.

In addition to the Sun and Moon keeping time, the star constellations appeared, or adopted the same position in the sky at the same time each year thus reinforcing the cyclical nature of life. If you look up at the stars you know spring has arrived when the throng of winter constellations moves off towards the horizon. In March and April the nights are not so cold and looking at the spring constellations can provide a much-needed tonic.

On a clear night one March, Red and I were out for the whole night. I wrapped up warm and lay back on my sun lounger. Red snuggled up close and we looked at the arc of Taurus, Orion and Canis Major. Ursa Major (the Big Dipper) was already halfway up in the northwestern sky and Leo, the Lion roared just as high in the east. I cast my eyes down near the horizon, a little northeast, and spotted the distinctively orange star, Arcturus twinkling madly. This springtime star is still quite low in March. Up from Arcturus I saw the constellation of Cancer, the Crab. It is faint but if the sky is dark you will see an unmistakable fuzzy patch of light at the centre of the constellation: the Beehive cluster.

The Beehive lies exceedingly close to the centre of the zodiac, the zodiac being that part of the sky the Sun, Moon and planets travel across when observed from Earth. The bright planets often travel near or even right through the Beehive cluster as if feeding from a little celestial pot of honey. Several of the winter constellations are barely past their peak and can observed before they finally depart.

A Rare Sight In The Sky

Around 11.30 pm, one Thursday evening I was lying on my sun lounger with Red in my garden. It was a dark night and I happened to glance north and I could hardly believe my eyes. The northern sky was dancing with a green eerie light. I looked again and shouted 'Red, look at this!'. Red jumped up and looked, his jaw wide open in amazement, he's a real astronomer!

A gradual brightening of the sky eventually reached a sixth of the way up from the horizon. Greenish tentacles surged upwards like silent ghostly figures and at the height of the display, a shimmering curtain of light hung from the sky, its pattern changing from second to second. The event lasted about fifteen minutes.

This spooky glow of activity was the Northern Lights or the Aurorae Borealis. The Northern Lights, called the Southern Lights or Australasia Borealis in the Southern Hemisphere are great celestial displays of light usually only visible within the

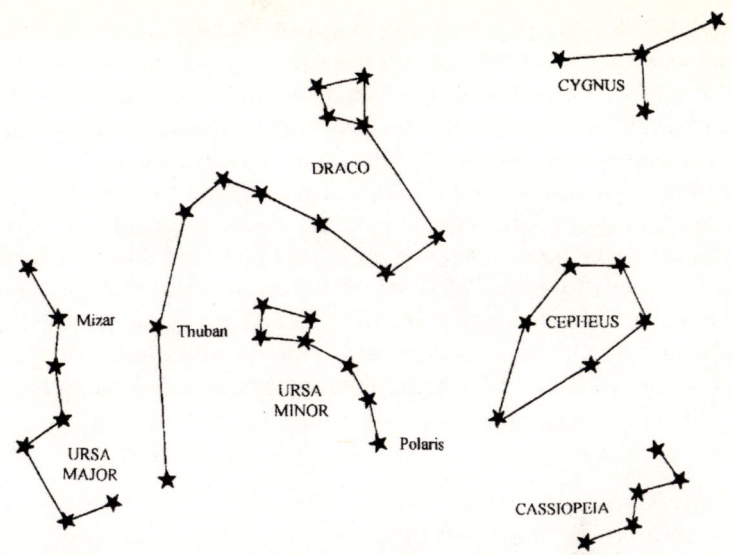

Fig 3 THE NORTHERN SKY The celestial pole is in the direction of the star Polaris. The celestial sphere revolves around this point in the sky.

Arctic circle: Alaska, Canada, Siberia, though they may be seen occasionally from the northern tip of Scotland. Yet here they were visible from central England!

Aurorae occur when charged particles in the solar wind, material ejected from the Sun spirals down along the Earth's magnetic field lines and strikes molecules in the atmosphere, causing them to emit light. Aurorae are usually seen near the Earth's northern and southern magnetic poles, but can be seen at much lower latitudes in the event of strong solar outbursts. The events are sporadic and could not accurately be predicted. Today however, advance warning may be given. Our technology can detect occurrences of mass ejections from the Sun. When one occurs, its strength is rated and a couple of days elapse before aurorae may be seen on Earth. One never knows exactly when the aurorae will be seen. You just have to go out and look at the night sky but statistically, your chance of observing aurorae is increased, armed with data from solar probes.

The aurorae I observed resulted from a mass solar ejection during the peak of the Sun's eleven-year sunspot cycle. The Sun follows an eleven-year cycle where dark regions on its surface, many times bigger than the Earth appear: sunspots. An increase in sunspot activity means an increase in solar activity. During the 1989 sunspot maxima, the plasma ejected from the Sun and which reached Earth on March 13th was so energetic it knocked out the power grid supplying most of Quebec and nearly swamped the entire United States' power grid.

Another interesting sight at springtime is zodiacal light. It can occasionally be seen soon after the Sun has set and takes the form of a cone of diffuse light glowing above the western horizon. This odd pearly light is caused by thinly spread particles of dust in the plane of the inner solar system which are illuminated at this time of year by the light of the Sun. It is faint but worth looking for.

Meteors

On any Moonless night you can see shooting stars or meteors. At certain times of the year, they are much more numerous. A meteor is the visible effect of a small particle, about the size of a grain of sand entering the Earth's upper atmosphere at speeds in excess of a thousand miles an hour. Friction between the small particle and molecules of the atmosphere heat the surrounding air causing it to glow. Often the glow persists for several seconds leaving a trail of light and it is this light we see as a shooting star.

These tiny particles of matter or meteoroids orbit the Sun. Most originate in comets and are released as the Sun heats up a comet's nucleus. Streams of particles released from a comet continue to orbit the Sun in similar orbits to the comet that gave rise to them. If the orbit of the stream intersects that of the Earth we may see a meteor shower. As the Earth reaches the same part of its orbit at the same time each year, the same meteor showers will occur around the same dates.

We can therefore predict when meteor showers will occur. On the evening of April 21st we have such a meteor shower: the Lyrids. Meteors appear to radiate from one region of the sky known as the radiant. The Lyrids radiate from the area between Lyra and Hercules and can give a fine display. The hourly rate is usually around ten. The Lyrids meteor shower lasts around four days and peaks just after the second day. Of course, rogue meteors can be seen any night of the year streaking across the sky. And yes, I always make a wish when I see a shooting star. You should make a wish too. If you believe with all your heart your wish will come true!

April

Daytime jaunts in the countryside in April have a way of getting out of hand. The land is especially inviting and I end up going far a field and through a greater variety of surroundings than I expected, especially if Red is with me.

In the daytime, Red leads the way. If you take your 'pet' into rural areas remember the country code. Red is well trained having spent his life walking by my side over all terrains. Red is also a smart dog. Indeed in their natural habitat animals are a lot smarter than humans. While walking, Red and I often engage in deep conversation. I say to Red 'Red, look at that interesting cloud formation. That is caused by a rising thermal, you know'. Red looks and nods in agreement. He is a scientific dog!

Fig 4
ARCTURUS is second in brightness only to Sirius

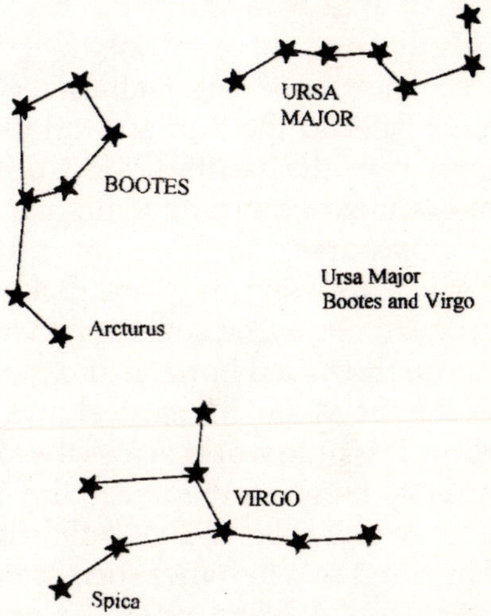

BOOTES

URSA MAJOR

Arcturus

Ursa Major
Bootes and Virgo

VIRGO

Spica

The April sky is not as dark as the winter sky and the stars are not so bright. But the brute cold of winter has gone and the summer midges are not yet making a nuisance of themselves. Surprisingly, we have the odd very bright 'blazer', for example Regulus high in the south, Arcturus more than a third of the way up in the eastern sky and Spica somewhat lower in the southeast. One could argue these bright stars stand out with even more individuality than many of winter's bright sights. But the spring constellations on the whole are dimmer and provide less competition. Regulus also stands out because of its special position. It is a first magnitude star close to the ecliptic, the midline of the zodiac.

Planets

'Twinkle twinkle little star, how I wonder what you are, up above the world so high, like a diamond in the sky.' is an old familiar rhyme. Stars are essentially a point source of light and the starlight we see on Earth is often refracted and defocused by atmospheric turbulence. This is why stars twinkle or scintillate. Planets, on the other hand have just enough 'angular size' and their light is much less ruffled by our moving air. Planets therefore, as a rule, do not twinkle.

The word planet means wanderer and was so named by the Greeks. Because planets are not (apparently) fixed objects like the stars they appear to wander across the sky. Once you learn to identify a planet, there are only five visible to the naked eye, you will recognise them without the aid of a star chart. Mercury is the closest planet to the Sun and orbits the Sun inside the Earth. Mercury is an elusive little world, difficult to glimpse and is visible at evening or morning twilight always close to the Sun.

Suburban areas may have difficulty spotting Mercury because you need a horizon free of obstruction and street light pollution. Given good observing conditions Mercury may be seen skirting a clear unobstructed horizon and glowing with a faintly pinkish hue. Like the Moon, Mercury shows phases and it is interesting to follow this little world across the sky. Mercury is New when it lies exactly between the Earth and Sun. As it moves along its orbit more and more of the sunlit side becomes turned towards the Earth and so it becomes successively a crescent, a half, a three quarters and full Mercury. However when full, Mercury is actually behind the Sun and therefore difficult to see. The phases are only visible through a pair of binoculars or a telescope.

All the planets in the solar system, at some time move behind the Sun or are close to the Sun. When this happens, the glare of the Sun makes observation impossible. If Mercury is visible in spring it is a great time to observe the winged messenger of the Greek gods. Never look directly at the Sun and never look at the Sun through a pair of binoculars or a telescope. If you are looking for Mercury wait until the Sun has set. Mercury will still be there if your horizon is unobstructed.

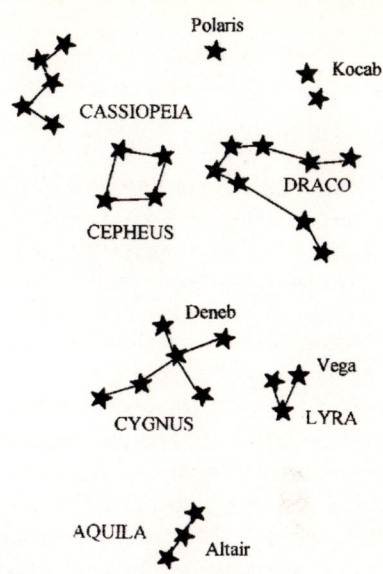

Fig 5 CEPHEUS AND CYGNUS Down from Cassiopeia lies Cepheus, Draco and Cygnus (the Swan). The stars of Cygnus look more like a cross than a bird and this is why people refer to it as the 'Northern Cross'.

May Sky

You will need quite a dark sky to see the May constellations well. However, there will not have been a great deal of movement during the month. The second meteor shower of the season occurs around May 4th: the Eta Aquarids. This is the southern hemisphere's richest shower but at northern temperate latitudes the Eta Aquarid never rises to a high altitude during the night-time. If we are lucky, we may see one meteor an hour. If you are holidaying in Spain or farther south around the Mediterranean you should see up to ten meteors an hour.

Astrologically, the vernal equinox sets the starting point of the zodiac. Traditionally the first sign of the zodiac is Aries. However, astronomically the vernal equinox now falls in the zodiac sign of Pisces. The zodiac is slipping by a small amount each year, approximately one degree every seventy-two years. This equinoctial slippage is caused by a motion of the Earth called 'precession'. It also alters the fabric of the zodiac. There are currently thirteen signs and not twelve signs of the zodiac. The thirteenth sign of the zodiac is Ophiuchus, the Healer or Serpent Bearer. Indeed several planets pass through a further three signs of the zodiac: Orion, Sextans and Cetus. Around March 27th a portion of the Sun actually spends time in Cetus. It could therefore be argued there are fourteen Sun signs and sixteen signs of the zodiac!

The cross quarter festival days were calculated by the Sun and the fixed zodiac signs. However, due to the precession they are now out of alignment. Bealtaine was calculated by determining the date on which the Sun is at fifteen degrees Taurus. It is a 'power point' of the zodiac as are all the fixed zodiac signs: Taurus, Leo, Scorpio and Aquarius. Taurus is one of the tetramorph figures of the Major Arcana. Tarot has a very close association with astrology.

Lunar Myths

Our relationship with the Moon has always been profound and intimate. The mystical Moon held sway over our ancestors with her magical and eternal beauty. Her dark face and changing moods plagued our forbears with doubt and foreboding while her shimmering light brought enchantment, happiness and romance. They knew the Moon's influence was great and her movements touched every aspect of their lives and their environment. Our ancestors slowly learned how to recognise the Moon's many faces and interpret her signs. Based on these observations, lunar folklore and myths were born.

The most interesting celestial object and one with the greatest influence on our lives today is still the Moon. The Moon is visible from bright city centres, changes 'shape' throughout each month and moves across the sky quickly. The word 'month' is derived from the word Moon. Many cultures believed if the New Moon came on Monday, (Moon-Day) it would be the unluckiest day there could be. Sailors thought if a large star or planet was seen close to the Moon, there would be wild weather coming and they called such a star a 'Moon dog'. Two New Moons in one month were said to predict a month's bad weather. Any New Moon on a Saturday or Sunday would predict rain and general bad luck.

Good luck will come your way if you first see the New Moon outside and over your right shoulder. A ring around the Moon means rain or snow. If you move to a new house or location during a waning Moon, it will ensure you never go hungry. In mediaeval times, 'Moon men' were thieves and highwaymen who plied their trade by night. The current term 'moonlighting' is similar, meaning to hold down an additional (usually illicit) night job. Many farmers believe crops sown near a Full Moon will be ready for harvest a month earlier than crops sown during a waxing Moon.

March Moon

The Full Moons of each month were allotted special powers and each given names. The March Moon is known as: Storm Moon, Moon of Winds, Plough Moon, Lenting Moon, Crow Moon. March is generally a blustery month. The old weather saying 'in like a lion, out like a lamb' is an apt description of March weather. March nature spirits are Air and Water, connected with spring rains and storms.

April Moon

April Moon names are Growing Moon, Hare Moon, Seed Moon, It is a time of unfolding leaves and flowers. The Floralia is still celebrated in many Central and Eastern European countries. It is a time to honour the goddess of flowers. People dress in gaily-decorated costumes and wear flowers in their hair. Secretly delivering baskets of flowers on May Day is a remnant of this old festival.

May Moon

May Moon names are Merry Moon, Fright Moon, Frog Moon, Flower Moon. The Greek goddess Maia, the most important of the Seven Sisters from the Pleiades constellation and the mother of Hermes, gave the name to this month. Some form of this goddess's name was known to people from Ireland to as far away as India.

The Romans called her Maius, goddess of summer and honoured her at the Ambarvalia, a family festival for purification and protection of farmland. The Celtic cultures called May, Mai or Maj, a month of sexual freedom. Green was worn during this month to honour the Earth Mother.

Summer

Great is the sun, and wide he goes
Through empty heaven without repose;
And in the blue and glowing days
More thick than rain he showers his rays.

Robert Louis Stevenson

When I attended infant school, my teacher Miss Crossley asked the class a question 'Do you know what day it is today, children?'. 'Monday, Miss' we all shouted, confident we had the right answer. 'Yes it is Monday, but do you know what is special about today?'. We looked at each other dismally and replied 'Don't know, Miss'. Miss Crossley informed the class: today is June 21st, the first day of summer. It is the longest day of the year and therefore the shortest night of the year. Today is midsummer's day and tomorrow the Sun begins to wane and the nights grow longer until midwinter's day. 'Oh, ah eee' gasped the class of seven year olds. I thought for a moment and put my hand up 'Miss, Miss'. 'Yes?' 'How can it be the middle of summer and the beginning of summer all in one day?' I asked. Miss Crossley sighed and began to explain, only her voice drifted off into the far distance. Miss Crossley was a wonderful teacher and I learned so much about the world from her, most of which was not remotely related to the school curriculum.

My early insight prompted by Miss Crossley is interesting. However, let me say one thing first: we become adults and we accept without question life's anomalies, whereas children question, everything; verbally and physically. Let a toddler roam free and every parent will tell you 'they get into everything'. It is a poignant reflection on how modern educational values appear to discourage inquisitiveness in children and replace it with meaningless, angst ridden, memory tests. Miss Crossley realised this and taught me 'children are candles to be lit and not empty vessels to be filled'.

June 21st is midsummer's day and it is also the first day of summer. It is the day of the summer solstice. Our different ancestral cultures are responsible for this confusion. The solstices or quarter days come from separate traditions to those of the cross-quarter days. The solar astronomical solstices are both older and newer than the Celtic greater Sabbat days. Older in that they were the highly sophisticated preoccupation of the Megalithic people who pre-date the Celts, Romans and Saxons by thousands of years. And newer in that the Celts gave the old Megalithic 'religion' an actual ritual shape which has survived.

Megalithic and Roman peoples celebrated the solstice as the first day of summer. The Celts celebrated the summer solstice as midsummer's day or Litha. We celebrate both. Scratch the topsoil of western traditions and you at once hit the bedrock of Megalithic and pagan ancestry.

In the northern hemisphere summer officially begins around June 21st when the summer solstice occurs, but the date may vary by a day or so. The summer solstice occurs when the Sun reaches its most northerly point in the sky, directly overhead at the Tropic of Cancer, 23 degrees 27 minutes north latitude. In the northern hemisphere, it is the longest day of the year and marks the beginning of summer. In the southern hemisphere where the seasons are opposite to those of the northern hemisphere it is the winter solstice which occurs. Similarly, when the winter solstice takes place it is the shortest day of the year and indicates the beginning of winter in the northen hemisphere.

Customs

The Celtic day ended at Sunset and not at midnight as it does today. Calibrating old festival dates with modern dates is awkward and often the date of the eve and the festival day are both influential. In ancient times 'Eve' the ending of the day leading on to the festival day was quite important. A few hundred years ago, Midsummer's Eve was known as St. John's Eve after John the Baptist but the midsummer tradition stems from Megalithic and pagan times.

In England it was the custom on Midsummer's Eve to light large bonfires after the Sun had set. This served the double purpose of providing light and warding off evil spirits. It was known as 'setting the watch'. Streets were lined with lanterns and people carried lanterns pivoted at the top of poles as they wandered from one bonfire to another. The wandering bands were called a 'marching watch'. Often they were attended by Morris dancers and players dressed as a unicorn, a dragon, and hobby horse riders. Just as May Day was a time to renew the boundary on one's own property, so Midsummer's Eve was a time to mark or ward the boundary of the city.

Customs surrounding Midsummer's Eve are many. Young folk would stay up throughout the whole of this shortest night. Some might spend time keeping watch in the centre of a circle of standing stones, which would result in either madness or the power of inspiration to become a great bard. Midsummer Eve was the night when the serpents rolled themselves into a hissing, writhing ball in order to engender the 'serpent's egg', 'snake stone', or 'Druid's egg'.

Snakes were not the only creatures active on Midsummer's Eve. This night was second only to Halloween for its importance to the 'little folk', who especially enjoyed roaming on a fine summer's night. In order to see the little folk, you had only to gather fern seed at the stroke of midnight and rub it onto your eyelids. To avoid being led astray by pixies, one carried a bit of rue in one's pocket. Failing this, you would turn your jacket inside out and if this fails, cross a stream of 'living' (running) water to keep safe from any malevolent power. Other customs included decking the house or front door with birch or fennel. Five plants were thought to have special magical properties on this night: rue, roses, St. John's wort, vervain and trefoil.

Shakespeare's 'A Midsummer Night's Dream' passes on this Eve. The drama is played out at the height of summer madness when pixies and fairies roam freely. The bard blends and intertwines four plots together where imagination and rationality become blurred. The timeless appeal of this play with its accent on the nature of love, reality, the status quo and social order, can be explained by its embryonic echoes of the recurring mania on Midsummer's Eve.

Pagan tradition sees Litha as the beginning of the Holly King's reign. This event is usually depicted by a battle between the God of the waxing year, the Oak King, and the God of the waning year, the Holly King. The two brothers each represent the light and dark halves of the year, respectively. On this day, the Oak King must give way to his twin, the Holly King, whose reign will continue until the winter solstice, when the Oak King is reborn. It is important to note the separation of the light and dark halves of the year have nothing to do with good and evil. Light signifies growth and expansion; dark means withdrawal and rest. Both are necessary.

In rural areas, a solar wheel would be set ablaze and rolled down a hill as a symbol of the Sun's power. Druids gathered mistletoe in the oak groves. Mistletoe without the berries was viewed as an amulet of protection. Older amulets were cast into the midsummer Sabbat fire, with the respect due to them and the ashes scattered on the land to make it fertile.

Stonehenge

Midsummer Megalithic customs are best observed at stone circles in alignment with the solstice. Red and I have visited Stonehenge on the Eve and day of the summer solstice. The solstice sunrise appears on the horizon in direct alignment with Stonehenge's massive heel stone. There is little doubt the builders of Stonehenge used it to mark the solstice as a special day. By counting the days between this annual alignment they determined the length of the year. This is one of the most outstanding features of this cosmic monument constructed during the same era as the Great Pyramid of Egypt.

Watching the Sunrise from inside the stones was a surreal experience. The early morning shadows were long and sharp. As the shadows grew and became stronger my mind drifted back to a time thousands of years before and I wondered who had built this remarkable monument. I tried to visualise these people standing beside me and I felt their presence. I was dumbstruck. The distant souls who constructed Stonehenge were really just like you and me. They could have been my aunty or the person serving breakfast at the fast food restaurant on the A36 road. We live in a different era to that of 5000 years ago but the human condition has not changed. Society changes, technology changes, material artifacts change, but at its most basic, emotionally, psychologically, spiritually, the human condition has not changed. We have not changed. I say to Red: 'Red, we have not changed'. Red contemplates for a moment and nods!

When we stand in ancient monuments or become lost in a work of art we are connecting with something much greater than ourselves. Whether it be Stonehenge, the 17 000 year old cave paintings at Lascaux in southern France or your one-year old's first finger painting. We do not live through islands of time separated from one era to the next. We are connected through time when we sense the deeper structures that underlie the facade or the superficiality of things.

For many years, visitors to Stonehenge on the eve of the summer solstice were denied access by English Heritage and the National Trust, the bodies responsible for the site. The law of aggravated trespass introduced primarily to support the Trust, strengthened this prohibition. Recently, access by small groups of approved visitors has been allowed. You may not agree with me but I believe we all have as much right to visit Stonehenge on the morning of the summer solstice, as do the quangos, bureaucrats and philistines who sit for most of the year in air-conditioned offices in London! I, and millions of others do not want to harm this unique and magnificent site. We do not want to live in an island of time but connect through time and join with those who stood before at the solstice sunrise.

I hope the final plan for Stonehenge will be worthy. An independent body, incorporating a wide cross section of the community, both lay people and experts should be established to manage this cosmic site. Money from the national lottery, private donations or the public purse ought to be provided and no expense spared. I am not against entrepreneurial initiatives but would not wish to see a commercial, profit driven operator managing Stonehenge. Disneyfication is appropriate in its place!

Twilight

The nights in June are not really so dark and observation is limited. Red and I are content to enjoy the glorious twilights, interesting cloud formations and long evening walks. Midsummer is the time when all is flourishing. Flowers smell their sweetest, trees are at their greenest and it is the time that nature's lavishness is most acutely perceived. My family often visit Scotland around this time of year staying at Hopeman, a small harbour village on the shores of the Moray Firth. At this latitude (58 degrees North) it doesn't really go dark at all in June. It is not quite the land of the midnight Sun but it is the next best thing.

After the Sun sets, when does twilight end and night begin? Night never arrives at all at high northern latitudes, above seventy-five degrees, in June. The northern polar region is bathed by perpetual daylight. However, further south, twilight depends not only on your latitude but also on which kind of twilight you mean. 'Civil' twilight ends when the Sun is six degrees below the true horizon. Under a clear sky this is when most outdoor activities need artificial lighting. Nautical twilight ends when the Sun descends to twelve degrees below the horizon. A sea horizon ceases to be visible well enough for a sailor to use a sextant to take navigational sightings. Astronomical twilight ends when the Sun descends to eighteen degrees below the horizon. This is when the last trace of the Sun's afterglow supposedly disappears. In June the Sun's afterglow is present throughout the night.

There is therefore not much time to observe the night sky in June. But there is a danger of leaping too quickly across the sky from eye catching Arcturus to Spica high in the southwest to Scorpius in the southeast or the Summer Triangle in the east. The brave Lion, Leo is dropping in the west while the noble Eagle, Aquila is ascending in the east. Ursa Major wheels high in the northwest and bright Antares is coiling up from the southeastern horizon. Libra is centred almost halfway from Antares to Spica. It is the void between the stars, as Cancer is sometimes called the void between Pollux and Regulus.

July Sky

The stars on a dark summer night convey a sense of timelessness. Red and I are usually in a good mood at the refreshing cool end of a warm summer day. Or we are caught up feeling summer is endless, the peak of the year when little changes for weeks on end. If we are lucky enough to have a Moonless night and are away from bright lights, we confront a cosmic structure so vast in space and time our minds turn to thoughts of infinity and eternity. I allude to the luminous arch spanning the eastern sky on July evenings, the glowing band of the Milky Way. This is the densely star-packed disk of our home galaxy, seen edge-on from our vantage point inside it. The Milky Way galaxy is home to our Solar System together with at least 200 billion other stars and their planets, thousands of star clusters and gaseous nebulae. All of the objects within the Milky Way orbit a common centre of mass called the Galactic centre.

As a galaxy, the Milky Way is actually a giant, its mass being equal to one trillion Suns and its diameter about 100 000 light years. Light travels at a constant speed of 180 000 miles per second and a light year is the distance light travels in one Earth year, approximately: 6 000 000 000 000 miles. Our Milky Way belongs to the Local Group of galaxies, a small group of three large and over thirty small galaxies. The Milky Way is the second largest galaxy after the Great Galaxy in Andromeda, which is around two and a half million light years distance and is our nearest large galaxy. A number of faint galaxies lie much closer. Several of the dwarf Local Group members are satellite galaxies or companions of the Milky Way. The closest is around 80 000 light years distance and is in fact interacting with our Milky Way galaxy, which is very gradually swallowing it up.

The Solar system is situated within the outer regions of a galactic spiral arm about twenty light years above the equatorial plane and 28 000 light years from the galactic centre. Viewed from Earth the luminous band of the centre of the Milky Way (the galactic equator) spans the constellation of Sagittarius and touches both of its neighbour constellations Scorpius and Ophiuchus. The Milky Way is an awesome sight to behold on a clear dark night. Unfortunately the glare from light pollution diminishes its splendour. Imagine travelling back to prehistoric times when our global population numbered under a million and no sky pollution existed. What a sight our forbears saw, a giant ghostly cloud, whose power and enormity could barely be comprehended and whose distance unimaginable.

Meteor Shower

A rather dim meteor shower peaks around July 29th, the Northern Delta Aquarids. The Aquarids are rich in faint meteors making it suitable for binocular observation although a few brighter meteors exist to make naked eye observation worth the effort. A more southerly site is better than the British Isles. If the sky is dark and there is no Moon you will see several meteors on a good night.

First Harvest

On August Eve, the Eve of the first harvest of the year, our ancestors honoured the great Earth Mother for her fertility and thanked the Sun Father for warmth. We have only recently lost this celebration as a meaningful festival, which persisted right up to the 1950's. Modern farming methods, pesticides, herbicides, genetic hybrid seed and rapid global transportation now provide plenty all year round. In past times a bad harvest meant a lean year. A good harvest meant plenty for all and an easy winter.

Not only did our Megalithic and pagan ancestors celebrate the first harvest, every culture across the northern temperate zones on Earth did so. The Harvest has great powers as it is the culmination of the hopes and dreams of the past season. It is a time of anticipation, planning for the dark season to come and for putting aside seed to plant in the following spring.

August Bank holiday is a poor substitute for the ancient, wonderful, first harvest holiday. I make a point of attending a Harvest service each year whether it be the first or the second (Harvest Home) where children offer a basket of fruit and vegetables to distribute within their community. I am aware most people in the West are not in dire need of fruit and vegetables. Indeed, much of the produce in the Harvest basket, these days, are in the form of cans and pre-packed supermarket items. That does not matter because it is the act of giving and receiving which is important. It is the act of giving and receiving which makes us human, giving of ourselves for the benefit of others, the benefit of the wider community.

My favourite Harvest hymn is 'We plough the fields and scatter the good seed on the land' by Matthias Claudius, which I also sing in the bath. '.. He paints the wayside flower, He lights the evening star..' Harvest Moon, Full Moon occurs around the autumnal equinox (September 21st). During this season, the Moon rises at a point opposite to the Sun and a few minutes later each night, affording on several successive evenings a Moonrise close to Sunset time and strong Moonlight almost all night.

Solar Eclipse

A total solar eclipse is a rare event unless you are prepared to travel the globe to observe one. On average, two occur each year. Two total solar eclipses occurred over the British Isles in the last century. I did not attend the first eclipse on June 29, 1927. I did attend the second eclipse on August 11th, 1999. The orbits of the Earth, Moon and Sun lie in the same plane and from time to time the three bodies are perfectly in line. When the Moon passes between the Earth and the Sun a solar eclipse occurs. Not all eclipses are total, some are partial where only a percentage of the solar disc is obscured by the Moon.

During a total eclipse we are able to glimpse for a brief moment the outer part of the Sun's atmosphere which cannot normally been seen. I observed the 1999 eclipse from a hill top seven miles from Truro in Cornwall. Cloud intermittently hid the Sun from view but I did glimpse the corona and chromosphere. It was a strange and eerie feeling when darkness fell over the land at 11.11 am on 11.8.1999. The next total solar eclipse in Britain occurs on September 23rd 2090. The path of totality passes over Cornwall, Devon and the south coast of England.

A Night Under the Heavens

An event I look forward to each year occurs around August 12th, the Perseids meteor shower. The Perseids are active between July 17th and August 24th and have become the single most exciting and dynamic meteor shower in recent times. The Perseids appear to come from an area of the sky between Cassiopeia and Perseus and are thus known as the Perseids. The Perseids are known to have been active for at least two thousand years and were traditionally known as The Fiery Tears of St Lawrence, St Lawrence's Day being August 10th.

The progenitor comet responsible for the meteor stream which produces this annual shower is comet 109P/Swift-Tuttle discovered independently in 1862 by the American astronomers Lewis Swift and Horace Tuttle. Usually over seventy meteors an hour may be observed and often the number is much higher.

Fig 6 CASSIOPEIA AND PERSEUS
Perseus can easily be located just below the 'W' of Cassiopeia.

I organise a field trip each year for around thirty people to observe the Perseids meteor shower. We travel to Anglezarke moor on the western flank of the Rossendale Fells in Lancashire and spend the night observing.

I have organised these trips for about fifteen years. I hire minibuses, a van and set up camp on the moors. The observation session is more than solely looking for meteors. The evening brings everyone closer to the cosmos, closer to nature and closer to each other. No comforts other than warm clothing, low wattage torches and binoculars are allowed. We use campfires for warmth (and effect) but resort to primer stoves to cook breakfast and to heat soup. Housewives, househusbands, office workers, group leaders, teenagers, grandmothers, i.e. you and me attend these field trips and we have a wonderful time. Women always outnumber men and most members of the group do live in towns or cities. Many are not accustomed to the blackness, openness and stillness of a night on the moors. Red and I are not scared of the dark, well, not most of the time but I can assure you when lying on one's sun lounger in the pitch-black of night several people become a little scared. They hear strange noises (wildlife) and do not want to be left alone. After reassurance, some settle down while others sit by the campfires and watch the sky from there.

August nights are clear, dark and reasonably warm. We watch the Sun set and we witness the Sunrise. Many of us are emotional at Sunrise. We share an activity our ancestors shared every clear night and we connect with nature in a way so hard to describe. We gather to observe meteors, which we do and they are exciting to see but just as exciting is being out under the stars together. We experience the sounds, smells and sights of nature without the darkness of reason.

Before the first glimmer of dawn twilight, we gather around the campfires to eat a hearty breakfast. The tension of the night is gone and everyone is relaxed, all the psychological barriers are down. There is something almost transcendental sharing this time together in this way. Life is all about sharing and the warm feelings generated from the simple act stay with one forever. I can only tell you how much I enjoy it.

Spending a night outdoors on the moors away from familiar surroundings changes people. Maybe just for an hour, maybe forever. The outdoors is a great social leveller. When you are close to nature it does not matter if your home is a mansion or a hovel. You are 'naked' and sharing the same experience. Your worries disappear. Who cares about the insurance, your career or problems with interior decorators when you are under the stars for a night watching seventy meteors an hour whiz by?

Look back on your life. Look deep into your soul and tell me of the moments that mean something to you. I will tell you it is not the day you made that insurance payment or had double-glazing or central heating installed. It is the day you fell in love, gave birth or became a father or were at the side of a friend or close relative who died. It is the day you marvelled at the Sun rising or became hypnotised by the distant horizon. It is the day you encountered a religious, spiritual or transcendental experience. It is the day when something deep within awakened, touched your consciousness and changed your life forever. I believe with all my heart, these are the important things in life, not peer group pressure or unrealistic life goals.

As an educator, I learned about group dynamics. One system describes a process of storming, norming, performing and mourning. Stages of human interaction which occur within any learning group also occur in our little group when we observe the Perseids. Group members meet, joke and jostle for recognition, they are storming. The group normalises. The group performs or interacts satisfactorily and in the morn, we mourn when we say goodbye.

Red

Many people are not animal people and when they first see Red by my side are a little apprehensive. Red is smart, he is my companion and he his a loner. He is his own dog! I say to Red 'Red you are a smart dog'. Red looks at me rather indignantly as if to say 'I know!'. He doesn't jump or bark unnecessarily at strangers. Red instinctively seems to know when a 'non animal person' is around and he makes allowances.

I recall an incident with a teenage man who was obviously a non-animal person. Red and I were resting by a dry-stone wall in Rivington near Anglezarke. The man, not dressed for hiking, walked by and asked for a drink of water. He stood back, keeping an eagle eye on Red. I offered him a can of carbonated beverage and I think he felt obliged to acknowledge Red's existence. He plucked up courage and stroked Red. He had the shock of his life. 'He's warm!' the man cried in utter amazement. He had never touched an animal before in his entire life and I assume by his reaction, he thought Red would be stone cold to the touch. He walked with us a while touching Red and talking to him. I hope he has overcome his animal anxiety.

Lunar Eclipse

My first son was born in September and my second son two years later in September. I had been visiting 'mother and baby' at hospital (Park Royal in North London) on September 16th and I walked home by the Grand Union canal. It was around 10.00 pm and I remembered the total eclipse of the Moon. I looked up towards London and sure enough, the Moon was in the shadow of the Earth and a lovely coppery colour.

A total lunar eclipse occurs when the Earth passes directly between the Sun and the Moon causing the Earth's shadow to fall upon the lunar surface. This can only happen at Full Moon. The Moon's colour changes from the very bright white to a dim, orange, coppery colour. Sunlight is bent and refracted in the

Earth's atmosphere and the colour of the Moon during a total eclipse is the colour of a thousand Sunsets on Earth. You can see the curve of the Earth as the shadow advances across the Moon's surface. A lunar eclipse usually occurs within two weeks either side of a solar eclipse. The period of totality can last over an hour because the Earth's shadow is much larger than the diameter of the Moon.

The evening each of our children arrived home from the maternity unit my wife and I wrapped them in a blanket and ventured out into the night to feel the presence of the stars. We had an overpowering urge to show the cosmos to them. They are now adults and know the sky intimately just as one knows the way around one's hometown.

Lunar Myths

The Moon of Midsummer is known as the Honey Moon because mead made from fermented honey was drunk on wedding nights as an aphrodisiac. The month of June is a favourite month to be married and hence the term, 'going on honeymoon'. We thus observe the roots of modern day marriage practices in their pagan ground.

If the New Moon is seen for the first time straight ahead it predicts good fortune until the next New Moon. Wood cut at the New Moon is hard to split. If it is cut at the Full Moon it is easy to split. Grass crops should be sown at the Full Moon so the hay will dry quickly. In Wales, fishermen avoid the Moon line, or the Moonlight showing on the water when setting out to sea, as they consider crossing this, bad luck.

Many cultures felt it was extremely unlucky to point at the Moon and curtsies to the Moon would bring a present before the next change of Moon. Originally, the term Moonstruck meant chosen by the goddess. These people were considered to be blessed. If a person were born at a Full Moon, he or she would have a lucky life.

June Moon

June Moon names are: Mead Moon, Lovers' Moon, Honey Moon, Strawberry Moon, Rose Moon. The original Roman name for this month was Junonious, after the Great Mother Goddess Juno, her counterpart among the Greeks being Hera. The summer solstice has been and still is important to many religions and cultures around the world. Not only was it sacred in its relation to goddesses of fertility, marriage, and love, but also it was considered to be a time when fairies, elves, and many other supernatural beings were out in great numbers. Tides of psychic energy flow freely, enabling even the most staid of people to experience unusual happenings.

The Full Moon festival of Edfu in Egypt honoured the goddess Hathor. The cow horns on her head represented the Crescent Moon. Every year at the New Moon the statue of Hathor was taken from her temple at Dendera and transported by boat to the temple of the god Horus at Edfu, arriving on the Full Moon. This festival celebrated the sexual union of the two deities. It was a time of great festivities and very likely, human marriages, since it was considered a period of good luck.

The Celtic deity of Cerridwen and her cauldron may have originally been associated with the summer solstice. Cerridwen of Wales was a Dark Moon goddess; her symbols were the cauldron, grain, and the Moon.

July Moon

July Moon names are: Hay Moon, Wort Moon, Blessing Moon, Fallow Moon, Thunder Moon. At first the Romans called this month Quintilis, but later renamed it Julius after Julius Caesar. The Greek Olympiad was held for about a week in July. This festival, in honour of Zeus, consisted of competitions in athletics, drama, music, and other activities. During the time of the Olympiad all participants were given safe conduct to and from the games. Their constant petty Greek squabbles were put aside. A victory in the Olympiad was a great achievement both for the individual and for their city.

In Japan, the Full Moon of July saw the O-Bon or Festival of Lanterns. This was a combination of Buddhist and Shinto beliefs honouring the dead. Homes, tombs and ancestral tablets were thoroughly cleaned. Altars and shrines were decorated. The gardens were hung with lanterns to light the way of the dead so they could join with their families for the three-day ceremony. The Egyptian year was measured against the Nile and its yearly fertile floods. The Egyptian New Year fell in July, as did the Opet Festival. which commemorated the marriage of Isis and Osiris. Their sexual union was said to bring good luck to all people. About the same time in Rome, the love of Venus and Adonis was celebrated.

August Moon

August Moon names are: Corn Moon, Barley Moon, and Harvest Moon. August, originally called Sextilis by the Romans was later named Augustus in honour of Augustus Caesar. August 1st is the Celtic feast of Lughnasadh, meaning the celebration of harvest and new grain for bread. In Old English this became Lammas or 'Loaf Mass'.

Three times during August the Romans honoured the god Vulcan: on August 17th at the Portunalia; on August 27th at the Volturnalia; and again on August 23rd at the Volcanalia. This last festival was held outside the city boundaries and was to ward off accidental fires, a real threat in such closely packed and fire prone towns. Vulcan was not the only deity honoured during these festivals. The goddess Juturna, deity of fountains and Stata Mater, who puts out fires were invoked as a counterbalance to Vulcan's fires and volcanoes.

The very early Greeks had a holy day for Hecate the Dark Mother on August 13th and ten days later, one for Nemesis the goddess who balanced the scales of justice with rightful revenge and punishment. In Rome, women who had prayers answered by Diana and Hecate marched by torch light to the temples of these goddesses. There they held a special ceremony for women only and gave thanks. In India today the Hindu people still honour the elephant headed god Ganesha, the deity who removes obstacles and brings good luck. Flowers and dishes of rice were set before his statues. However, it is considered unlucky to look at the Moon during this festival.

Autumn

Season of mists and mellow fruitfulness!
Close bosom-friend of the maturing sun;
Conspiring with him how to load and bless
With fruit the vines that round the thatch-eaves run;

John Keats

Autumn is my favourite season. Long shadows are cast by the low altitude of the Sun and the special quality of daytime Sunlight produces soft colours to enchant the mind. Autumn, like spring has its own individual earthy smell, ripened fruit, decaying leaves and the first fresh breezes of cold air. The night skies too are clear, transparent and dark. Perhaps I like autumn best of all the seasons for a deeper bio-psychological reason. I was born on October 28th, smack in the middle of the season. In case you didn't know, October 28th is St Jude's feast day. St Jude is the patron saint of helpless, hopeless and desperate cases. So now you know, I have always been a helpless, hopeless and desperate case. It is written in my stars!

The autumn equinox is a time where day and night are of equal length, after which the dark becomes dominant and we descend towards winter. The second harvest, Harvest Home has been gathered and the Sun is still warm. There is a week to go before Michaelmas (September 29th) and at this time of balance, of suspended activity, the veil between the worlds of the living and the dead are approaching their thinnest point in the year.

Astronomically the autumnal equinox is one of the two points where the Sun crosses the celestial equator. The Sun travels along the ecliptic (zodiac) and moves across the celestial equator from the northern to the southern hemisphere around September 21st. This marks the beginning of autumn in the northern hemisphere and spring in the southern hemisphere.

Our Celtic ancestors were not accomplished at calculating the exact date of the equinox and so celebrated this 'low day' on a fixed calendar date, September 25th, the Mabon Sabbat. The mediaeval Church Christianised this equinoctial time under the name of 'Michaelmas', the feast of the Archangel Michael. The Celtic Harvest Home represented autumn's height, a lesser

Sabbat and a low holiday. The festival involved the concept of sacrifice, one of symbolic sacrifice only, to honour the spirit of vegetation. Good luck harvest figures called 'corn dollies' were made each year, 'corn' referring to any grain: wheat, rye, or oats. The corn dollies were placed in large wicker baskets ready for the annual mock sacrifice. British folk tradition is full of mock sacrifices. In the case of the corn dollies or wicker-men, such figures were referred to in personified terms, dressed in clothes and addressed by name.

Fig 7 HARVEST CORN DOLLY Good luck harvest figures were made every year from corn husks.

Transformation

The Wheel of the Year turns, and old pagan philosophy teaches death is a natural function of the universe. Death is part of life, a dramatic change heralding the beginning of a new cycle, something to be celebrated at the proper time and not feared. Today we are always trying to find new and better ways to beat death. We will not succeed. It troubles me how society portrays death as such a terrifying experience and a taboo topic of conversation. We would certainly experience less emotional pain and suffering if death could be seen for what it is: a transformation, a passing of our physical presence and the culmination of our life's energy. Our life's energy remains in the cosmos as an echo of our presence in it and thus we will always maintain links with the living.

It was considered disrespectful to pass burial sites and not honour the dead. At this time of year, apples were placed on burial cairns as a symbol of rebirth and gratitude. Furthermore, it was a time to honour the elders who had devoted much time and energy to growth and development. As far as I am aware, Japan is the only nation that has a national holiday for the elderly. 'Respect for the Aged Day' is observed on September 15th.

Celtic folklore passed down in the oral tradition tells us the Sun god is seen as split between two rival personalities: the god of light and his twin or 'other self', the god of darkness, the Oak King and the Holly King. They are depicted as fighting seasonal battles for the favour of their goddess, the Earth who represents Nature. The god of light is always born at the winter solstice and his strength waxes with the lengthening days until the moment of his greatest power, the summer solstice, the longest day. His 'shadow self', the lord of darkness, is born at the summer solstice and in turn, his strength waxes with the lengthening nights until the moment of his greatest power, the winter solstice, the longest night.

The Western Church incorporated these myths into its own philosophy several centuries after the death of Christ. The mirror-birth pattern is strongest in the Christianised form of this pagan belief. Jesus, though identified with the Holly King is 'the light of the world'. His birth is celebrated at midwinter, at the winter solstice. John the Baptist on the other hand is identified with the Oak King but is the 'dark of the world' because his birth (not his death) is celebrated at midsummer: at the summer solstice.

In folk tradition derived from the older pagan strain, it is births, not deaths that are associated with the solstices. John the Baptist is the only saint in the entire Church hagiography whose feast day is a commemoration of his birth rather than his death. All other saints are commemorated on the anniversary of their death, because their death was really a 'birth' into the Kingdom of Heaven. But John the Baptist is the sole exception and is emphatically commemorated on the anniversary of his birth into this world. Although this makes little sense, viewed from a Christian perspective, it makes perfect sense from the viewpoint of ancient pagan symbolism.

Welsh Mythology

In Welsh mythology too, there is a vindication of the seasonal placement of the Sun god's death. Llew is the Welsh god of light and his name means 'lion'. The lion is often the symbol of the Sun god: Leo the Lion. He is betrayed by his wife Blodeuwedd into standing with one foot on the rim of a cauldron and the other on the back of a goat (Capricorn). It is the only way Llew can be killed and Blodeuwedd's lover Goronwy, Llew's dark self, is hiding nearby with a spear. But as Llew is struck he is not killed. He is instead transformed into an eagle. The Welsh myth concludes with Gwydion pursuing Blodeuwedd through the night sky, and a path of white flowers springs up in the wake of her passing, which we know today as the Milky Way. When Gwydion catches her, he transforms her into an owl, a symbol of autumn. While Llew and Goronwy represent summer and winter, Blodeuwedd herself represents both spring and autumn as patron goddess of flowers and owls respectively.

At this time of year it was common practice to walk over wild places and through forests gathering seedpods and dried plants. Some of these were used to decorate the home and others saved for herbal remedies and healing. Red and I walk over wild places occasionally, gathering seeds, berries and a variety of foliage. We make elderberry wine, elderflower wine earlier in the year, and the whole family like to press and dry flowers. Unfortunately, nature's abundance has diminished over the years. I say to Red 'Red, where have all the meadow species gone?' Red looks quizzical and shakes his head. Many areas we once roamed are now in private hands. Not an odious landlord but private utility companies and other organisations who have placed barbed wire and 'Keep Out' notices where once dry stone walling and stiles used to be. Hikers and ramblers have great respect for the countryside as do country people and the increasing closure of once open paths by various organisations, shows a really mean spirited attitude.

Speculators, planners and developers also transform many of our green treasures into barren, alien landscapes. One delightful area I roamed as a child has disappeared under concrete and tarmac. A natural spring cascaded down a ten-foot rock face into a large bulrush lake surrounded by ferns and heather. It was called 'Johnny's Hump'. The bulrush lake and an adjacent Bluebell wood attracted a myriad of wild life. Each season Miss Crossley took my class on a nature walk to this location. We learned the names of trees, plants, animals and insects. We sketched leaves, gathered stones and observed the little creatures. We experienced the profusion of nature first hand. When I visit the area now and look at what we have done, what we have done to our beautiful world, to our beautiful little blue planet I am overcome. I am not angry but my soul crumbles to dust.

September Sky

I particularly enjoy this time of year. The nights are cooler and dark enough for observing the heavens. The days are warm and the sunlight magical. Red and I spend a couple of nights out under the stars but we always walk for an hour each evening as darkness falls. Looking skyward we see the Summer Triangle is just as much an autumn triangle in that its long decline from zenith to the west occurs slowly. In reality, the Triangle consists of three bright stars from different constellations: Dened, in Cygnus; Vega, in Lyra and Altair, in Aquila. The other bright star to look out for is Arcturus.

At this time of year, birds begin their annual migration and the night sky is a hive of activity as large flocks appear silently above the horizon and locust-like, blot out the heavens for several minutes. Red and I are occasionally startled by a sort of baying sound, as lines of geese produce silhouettes across a silver Moon. After our walk, we sit close to the fire at home. The longer evening hours mean I catch up on unfinished work while sipping homemade elderflower wine. Red lies on the rug in front of the hearth, thinking. He is a thinking dog! I say to him 'Red we are so lucky to live in a part of the world where the seasons change so dramatically, each having its own type of beauty'. Red doesn't reply. He doesn't even move, but a slight flicker of his ear tells me he agrees with me.

Planets may be seen at any time of the year depending upon their position. After the Sun and Moon, Venus ranks third in brightness. It was given the name of the goddess of love because of its pure white colour, white being a virginal colour. The ancients believed there were two brilliant white planets: the morning star 'Phosphorus' visible close to dawn and the evening star 'Hesperus' visible at sunset. We now know they are one and the same planet but seen at different times of the year. Venus is the second planet from the Sun and therefore closer to the Sun than the Earth. Venus comes closer to the Earth than any other planet and at its brightest, has a magnitude of -4. Venus is sufficiently powerful to cast shadows on the Earth, on a Moonless evening. Just as the Moon and Mercury show phases, so does Venus, passing from New Venus to Full Venus returning to New Venus over (varying) periods of time.

Messages from the Heavens

The occasional, unexpected appearance of a comet has fascinated and frightened humankind for centuries. Ancient cultures regarded comets as bad omens or portents of impending disaster. Today, many people still believe comets are harbingers of change and mainstream science has now discovered some truth in ancient comet mythology: comets have, and may one day again portend disasters on Earth. We know comets are agglomerations of ice, rock and dust, several miles wide, left over from the formation of the solar system around four and a half billion years ago. The ice and rock core of a comet is called the nucleus. As a comet approaches the Sun, solar heat warms the nucleus. The ice in the nucleus begins to vaporise liberating ice-encrusted dust which is then pushed away from the nucleus by the solar wind, producing the distinctive 'tail' thousands, even millions of miles long.

Comets may have played a crucial role in the evolution of life on Earth. Shortly after the formation of the solar system, the Earth was bombarded by an ongoing hail of comets for a period of several million years. In addition to water ice and rocky material, many comets are known to contain complex organic molecules. These molecules may have been the seeds from which life on Earth arose, a theory known as panspermia. Comets have also destroyed life. It is now clear a comet collided with the Earth and sealed the fate of the dinosaurs some sixty-five million years ago. The comet's impact blasted dust into the upper atmosphere and ignited fires for thousands of miles around. Smoke and dust remained suspended in the atmosphere for years, blocking sunlight. Without sunlight, much of Earth's plant life died. In turn, the dinosaurs that fed on the plants died and the carnivorous dinosaurs which fed on those dinosaurs eventually died clearing the way for the emergence of mammals and eventually, ourselves.

Cometary collisions are not just a chapter of ancient history. In July 1994, fragments of a comet called Shoemaker-Levy 9 crashed into Jupiter creating huge black spots in the massive planet's atmosphere. The last largish comet to strike the Earth did so in 1908 at Tunguska, Siberia, destroying hundreds of square miles of forest. Had the comet arrived four hours later it would have destroyed the city of Helsinki and the surrounding area with great loss of life.

Comet Hale-Bopp was a spectacular comet seen in the Northern Hemisphere during the autumn of 1997. I observed Hale-Bopp every night when visible. Nearly everyone I know saw the comet and many gained a spiritual benefit from its encounter. Several acquaintances remarked how they believed the comet carried away the spirit of Princess Diana after her tragic and premature death. Several cults, Heavens Gate from California in particular, were 'comet-struck' and believed Hale-Bopp to be a celestial messenger. It is not difficult to see why comets achieve this effect and one can construe numerous meanings from unrelated data to confirm comet message theories.

Let us undertake such an exercise. Comet Hale-Bopp was discovered independently but simultaneously by Alan Hale in New Mexico and Thomas Bopp in Arizona, on July 23, 1995; an unusual coincidence in that the two locations of discovery occurred on the same day and both at the same exact latitude North: Cloudcroft, New Mexico 32 degrees North, 105 degrees West; Stanfield, Arizona 32 degrees North, 111 degrees West. The middle point between Arizona and New Mexico is Route 666, this highway is in New Mexico to the South, and Arizona to the North. 666 is mentioned in the Book of Revelations as the number of the Antichrist and is generally a number associated with the occult world. From simple unrelated data we can infer much meaning and if we continued would eventually build a complete philosophical theory of Being. Heavens Gate took their philosophical theory too far and so seriously, they took their own lives, believing comet Hale-Bopp concealed a spacecraft or portal which was the Gateway to an everlasting life.

The most famous comet of all is Halley's Comet, known since 1059 BC. Its most celebrated appearance in 1066 AD was seen before the Battle of Hastings. It was named after Edmund Halley who calculated its orbit and determined that the comets seen in 1531 and 1607 were one and the same object following a seventy-six-year orbit. Halley died in 1742 never living to see his prediction come true when the comet returned on Christmas Eve 1758. Five spacecraft from the USSR, Japan and Europe were launched to make a rendezvous with Halley's Comet in 1986. The nucleus of Halley is ellipsoidal in shape and measures approximately eleven by five by five miles.

October brings clear weather, crisp nights and sparkling skies. Absence of cold is one advantage and a beautiful, clear, transparent sky is a bonus. The westerlies clean the air and we have deep blue skies by day and great observing conditions by night.

Halloween

All Hallows, all Hallow's Eve, Hallow E'en, Halloween is positioned exactly opposite Bealtaine (spring) on the Celtic wheel of the year. Today, as much as ever, it is a night of incandescent jack-o-lanterns, apple bobbing, trick or treating, and dressing in costume. In past times, ghost stories were told, seances held, tarot cards read and descrying with mirrors undertaken. All

Hallow's Eve is the eve of All Hallow's Day, November 1st. The traditional celebration of this great pagan New Year festival begins as the Sun sets on October 31st. The holiday was not only a pagan festival but celebrated by many ancient and unconnected cultures. The Egyptians and pre-Spanish Mexicans celebrated this as a festival of the dead. However, modern traditions can be traced directly to our pagan ancestors and the eternal rhythms of the heaven.

Fig 8 THE NORTHERN SKY If we look at the northern sky in autumn we see the constellations are the same as those visible in spring but they have shifted in orientation by 180 degrees.

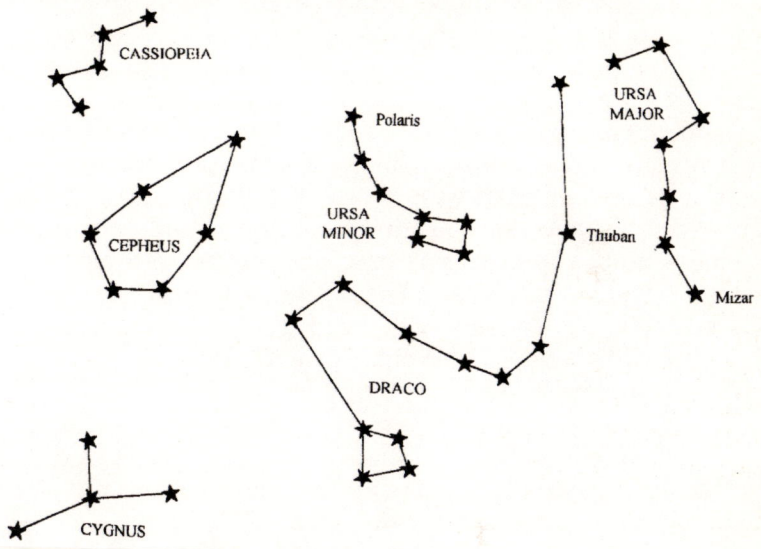

The Celts called Halloween 'Samhain' which means 'summer's end'. Not only is Samhain the end of summer/autumn it is the end of the old year and the beginning of the new. The New Year began with the onset of the dark phase of the year just as the new day began as the Sun set. There are many representations of Celtic gods with two faces and one must have held sway over Samhain. Its Greek counterpart, Janus straddled the threshold with one face turned toward the past in commemoration of those who died during the last year and one face gazing hopefully toward the future. These two themes, celebrating the dead and divining the future are inexorably intertwined in Samhain as they are in any New Year's celebration. On this night (Hollowe'en), our predecessors believed the dead could, if they wished, return to the land of the living to celebrate with their family, tribe, or clan. People have a tribal instinct and want to feel they belong to something that is greater than themselves.

Time

Our modern culture uses a linear concept of time. New Year's Eve is simply a milestone on a very long road that stretches in a straight line from birth to death and New Year's festival is a part of time. The ancient Celtic view of time was cyclical similar to the view held in Brahmanism, a Hindu system; in Buddhism; in Platonism and the Aboriginal peoples of Australia. In this framework, New Year's Eve represents a point outside of time where the natural order of the universe dissolves back into primeval disorder preparing to re-establish itself in a new order.

Samhain is a night existing outside of time and it may be used to view any other point in time. Ancient conceptions of the world, nature and man were based on the idea of cyclic time. Tribal myths were expressed in cosmic cycles and agricultural societies used a system of cosmic renewal through birth and rebirth. This theme of seasonal renewal was of great importance. Cyclical time is at variance with the idea of linear time typical of Judaism, Christianity, and Islam. However, as we have seen, no culture completely disregards the cyclic patterns of the seasons. Such patterns are engraved on our perception of the world.

Christian belief with its emphasis on the 'historical' Christ and his act of redemption 2000 years ago is forced into a linear view of time where 'seeing the future' is an illogical proposition. However, the mediaeval Church adopted Samhain's other motif: the commemoration of the dead. It could never be a feast for all the dead, only the blessed dead and all those hallowed (made holy) by obedience to God. Thus all Hallows or Hallowmas, later All Saints' and All Souls' Day emerged on November 1st. As a festival for the dead, it turned into a celebration of all the saints and martyrs of the Church introduced by Pope Boniface IV in the seventh century. It was originally celebrated on May 13th but was moved to November 1st by Gregory III in the eighth century. It seemed consistent for the Church celebration for the dead to coincide with the pagan celebration for the dead. All Saints' Day was followed by All-Souls' Day on November 2nd unless it was a Sunday, then it was November 3rd. 'Halloween', then is a Christian holiday, the Eve All Hallows' Day, but its lineage is shot through with many pagan threads.

The most famous icon of this High Holiday is the jack-o-lantern which originates from Scotland and Ireland. The lantern was used by people who travelled the road and it had a frightening face to intimidate spirits who might lead one astray. Set on porches and in windows, the lanterns cast the same spell of protection over the household. Pumpkins have now superseded the European gourd (a large hard-rinded fruit characteristic of the cucumber family) as the jack-o-lantern mantle, (an Americanisation).

The custom of dressing in costume and 'trick-or-treating' is of Celtic origin, and it survived in Scotland until recently. Again, we now practise the American import! This custom once was not relegated to children, but was actively indulged in by adults as the 'treat' required was often one of spirits (of the whisky variety). Roving bands would sing seasonal carols from house to house making the tradition very similar to Yuletide wassailing. The custom known as 'carolling', now connected exclusively with midwinter was once practised at all the major holidays.

The Apple

Bobbing for apples represents the remnants of a pagan 'baptism' rite called a 'seining'. The water filled tub is a latter day Cauldron of Regeneration into which the novice's head is immersed. After the Romans conquered Britain, two of their festivals were combined with the Samhain festival. The first of these was called Feralia and held in October to honour the dead. The other honoured Pomona, the Roman goddess of fruit and trees. Apples further became associated with Halloween because of this goddess; as well as the obvious reason i.e. the abundance of fallen apples in autumn.

Apples have long been treated as a token of love and fertility. Hebrew women who wanted children washed themselves in water mixed with the sap of an apple tree. 'Eternal Youth' was said to come to the Norse gods by the eating of apples. Bobbing for apples is an age-old tool for communicating with 'the other side' at Samhain and water represents a veil between this and the other world. Apples are associated with goodness and temptation. In the story of Adam and Eve, the apple signified hidden knowledge, which was forbidden to humankind. Snow White is tempted by an apple, and William Tell risks his son's life by shooting an apple off his head. Isaac Newton discovered the laws of universal gravitation when an apple fell on his head, (or so we are told). The 20th-century's most famous pop group, the Beatles named their recording label 'Apple'. The world's most exciting city, New York is called the 'Big Apple'.

Fig 9 THE PENTAGRAM
The pentagram is often considered as representing the microcosm and internal energies. Pentagrams are often found in nature, in flowers and crystalline forms, for example, and their shape can be used to draw a human figure in correct proportion. This was famously shown by master artist and inventor Leonardo Da Vinci (1452-1519) in his drawings made around 1492

The most distinguished icon of the pagan world and one still in use today stems from the humble apple: the five starred pentagram. Imagine the perfect apple, ripe and bursting with life. Slice the apple in half at the equator and it reveals a beautiful five point symmetry a star formed by the seeds inside: the pentagram. Fivefold symmetries are rarely found in non-organic life forms but are uniquely inherent to life: the human hand, starfish, flowers, plants and innumerable living things. The pattern of five exists even down to a molecular level and embodies the form, formation and essence of life. The pentagram is also a Jungian archetypal symbol with immense power over the unconscious mind.

Another date once worthy of planned celebrations was the astronomical cross quarter day, which occurred when the Sun reached fifteen degrees of Scorpio, an astrological 'power point' symbolised by the Eagle. This date was appropriated by the Church as the holiday of Martinmas, November 11th and considered to be a salutary time to take the thirteenth step: Transformation. In the Tarot, the thirteenth card of the Major Arcana is Death and is ruled by Scorpio. Samhain occurred in Scorpio. (It no longer does so due to an astronomical motion known as the precession of the equinoxes.)

The card of Death does not necessarily mean physical death but more fundamentally can be seen as an intense change or transformation. Something old must go to make room for something new. The magic of the time should be used to say good-bye to an old habit or addiction, an old relationship, or anything else it is time to leave behind. Even our New Year's resolution tradition stems from mystic pagan beliefs.

All of the Celtic cross quarter days are Fire Festivals. It is no coincidence that shortly after November 1st is Guy Fawkes Day, November 5th. Guy Fawkes tried to blow up Parliament when King James I was visiting the building. The gunpowder was already in place when the plot was discovered. Now Guy Fawkes Day is celebrated with fireworks, and bonfires are lit and effigies of Fawkes are burned all over England. This commemoration certainly invokes memories of the vegetable wicker-man, suggesting that far from triggering these fiery festivals Mr Fawkes' plot was a coincidental, additional excuse for them. That aside, I enjoy November 5th especially the fare: jacket potatoes, treacle toffee, parkin cake, toffee apples — and of course, Guy Fawkes Punch made from brandy. Red gets an extra bone but he does not care for the noise.

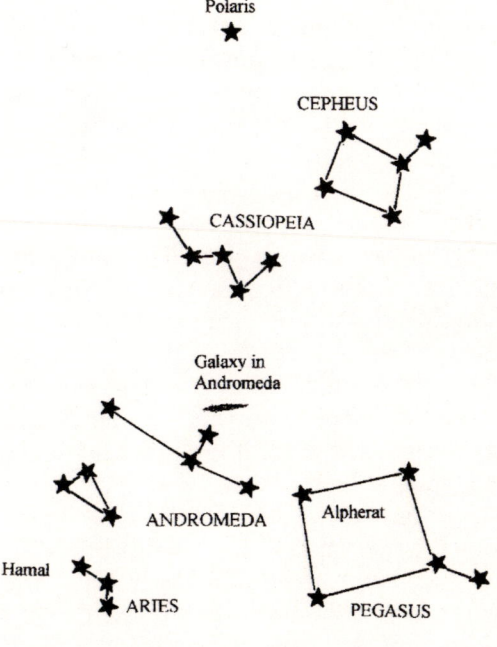

Fig 10 ANDROMEDA The Great Galaxy in Andromeda can be seen on a clear dark night. It is the most distant object visible to the naked eye at nearly three million light years distance

An Unusual Experience

Wrap up warm and make yourself comfortable for the nights are cold. Spend at least one night outdoors under the stars. Lie on your sun lounger with your head facing south so that you are looking north. Directly overhead and slightly to the left is the most distant object visible to the naked eye, the Great Galaxy in Andromeda. I drive an elderly Saab 900 car which has clocked over 200 000 miles (I use unleaded fuel with a catalytic converter fitted). It has an old style solid sunroof which pulls back, allowing Red to stick his head through. When I am driving at night and the sky is clear I pull the sunroof back fully, put on my hat and glimpse fleetingly at the stars above my head. Red jumps on the rear seat to get a better view. I feel the presence of the stars more this way, even though I am not directly observing them.

One November evening, I had given an interview with Steve Riches on the Steve Riches Show at BBC Radio for the Eastern Counties and I had to drive home from Northampton. The night was beautiful and clear so I took the dark, winding, country roads rather than the M1 motorway. Once in the country, I pulled my sunroof back and put on my hat. There was no Moon and all the stars in heaven shone brilliantly. I noticed the haze of Andromeda directly above my head and had to stop to take a look. A large expanse of short cut grass appeared on my right so I pulled over. I took my sun lounger, binoculars and Arctic winter clothing from the boot and settled down some fifty feet from the road to observe. Viewing conditions were perfect except for some minor illumination from a distant farmhouse, which continuously switched on and off its lights.

I let my eyes adjust to the darkness and gazed up at the Great Galaxy of Andromeda. Andromeda is the most distant object one can see with the naked eye at two and a half million light years distance. It is a huge galaxy, almost twice the size of our own Milky Way galaxy. Though faint, one is staggered by its size when viewed from Earth. Andromeda even at its immense distance is about four times the apparent diameter (angular size) of the Moon. I looked through my binoculars and the faint cloud took shape and form, an elongated giant Catherine wheel which would not fit into my binoculars' field of view.

Its true size and distance were not known until 1953 when the 200-inch Palomar telescope came on line. An 'island universe' over 150 000 light-years across whose light had been travelling through space for nearly three million years to reach Earth! I wondered about the light from Andromeda passing the Earth and continuing to travel until the end of time. Would another intelligent being (like myself) on some distant planet be looking at the very image I see before me in a million, 10 million or 100 million years time?

A car pulled in behind mine, two people hopped out and with a sense of purpose, walked towards me. I was a little curious. The two shadowy figures approached and one shone a light straight into my face. 'Good evening, sir. What are you doing ?' asked a police officer. 'Well, mmm, I'm just looking at Andromeda up there,' said I, pointing my index finger skyward and squinting from the dazzling torch. I don't think the officers believed me. 'I am an astronomer' said I. I explained where I had been and what I was doing. The officers checked my ID and car registration and when convinced I was not a burglar or a mad man, asked me to pack up and go home.

It transpired I had set up my sun lounger on the lawn of a large house and the occupiers called the police because some lunatic was lying on a sun lounger in the middle of the night on their lawn. I had mistaken their house for a distant farmhouse. It all turned out well in the end. The officers looked at Andromeda through my binoculars and we discussed the end of the universe. When you say you are an astronomer everyone asks the same question: 'Where does the universe end, and if it ends there, what is behind that?'

Mars is the fourth planet from the Sun and the first to lie beyond the orbit of the Earth. The planet is reddish orange in colour and hence its nick name 'the red planet'. It passes closest to Earth every two years (opposition) and this is when we see the planet clearly. Mars is unmistakable among the star fields because it moves through them quite quickly. At certain times, Mars also appears to move backwards in the sky. This retrograde motion is due to the Earth overtaking Mars in its orbit. The closer a planet is to the Sun the quicker it moves, plus its orbit is smaller so inner planets continually overtake outer planets.

Lunar Myths

Sailors believed if the Moon in the first or last quarter lay in nearly a horizontal position with the horns upward, the weather would be fine. Country people say the same type of Moon means good weather for twenty-eight days and yet others say the weather is more likely to change at the four quarters of the Moon than at any other time. Rain is coming when the Moon has a halo around it or when an outline can be seen between the horns of a waxing or waning Moon. One old legend says the Moon is everything that has ever been wasted on Earth: mis-spent time, squandered wealth, broken vows, unanswered prayers, fruitless tears, unfulfilled desires and intentions.

'To cry for the Moon' is an old saying meaning to crave or demand something that you can never have 'you might as well ask for the Moon'. The word moonshine has two meanings i) illegally distilled spirit, ii) total nonsense. A waning Moon was considered an unlucky time for a marriage or birth. In English, French, Italian, Latin, and Greek the Moon is feminine, but in all the Teutonic languages the Moon is masculine. In Sanskrit the word for the Moon is 'mas' which is masculine.

To the Chinese the Old Man in the Moon was Yue-lao and it was his duty to predestine the marriages of mortals. They say he tied the future husband and wife together with an invisible silk cord which never parted as long as they lived. Although the Koran expressly forbids worshipping the Sun or Moon, many Moslems still clasp their hands at the sight of a New Moon and offer a prayer.

September Moon

September Moon names are: Harvest Moon, Wine Moon, Singing Moon, Holy Moon, Wood Moon. September was the seventh month in the oldest Roman calendar. When other months were added to the seasonal calendar the name never changed. This month is the last of the reliable harvesting months in the northern hemisphere. Life is beginning to wind down in preparation for the dormant months that follow. The energy flows, from the autumn equinox through the winter solstice to the spring equinox are getting deeper and more hidden. The Dark Moon deities who represent the Underworld, death, reincarnation and deep spiritual mysteries now hold sway.

The Egyptian ceremony of 'lighting the fire' was a general festival of lights for all the gods and goddesses. Lamps of all kinds were set in front of deity statues and placed before the statues of ancestors. The Egyptian deity Thoth was the Lord of Holy Wards and inventor of the Four Laws of Magic. Thoth was a Moon god with the head of an ibis. As Supreme Magus or the ultimate Magician, he had control over the powers and attributes of the Moon.

In the old Incan Empire the Citua was held at the time of the New Moon nearest the autumn equinox. Everyone performed a ritual cleansing then smeared their faces with a paste of ground maize. There followed several days of feasting and dancing. This was a Moon festival in honour of Mama Quilla, the Moon goddess.

October Moon

October Moon names are: Blood Moon, Shedding Moon, Leaf Moon, Moon of Change. October or Octem, was the eighth month in the oldest Roman calendar. The 'Blood Moon' takes its name not from blood sacrifices but from the old custom of killing and salting down livestock before the winter months made it impossible to feed them. Only the choicest stock were kept alive through the cold season. Today, we subconsciously begin to make preparations for the coming winter at about this time. We check the antifreeze and tyres on the car, gather up garden waste and seal draughty spots around the house. We light a bonfire to burn garden and woodland debris.

The Greek festival of Thesmophoria came every year in honour of Demeter and was confined to women only. It was a three-day remembrance of Kor's return to the Underworld and at this festival the initiates shared a sacred barley drink and cakes. One feature of the Thesmorphoria was to act as a deterrent to offenders against the sacred laws and temples, especially the temples of Demeter and Artemis. It was believed anyone who broke these laws would die before the year ended.

In Tibet, the Buddhist Lent occurred along with the Descent from Heaven festival which celebrated the end of the rainy season.

November Moon

November Moon names are: Snow Moon, Dark Moon, Fog Moon, Mad Moon. November was the ninth month in the oldest Roman calendar. In the Celtic tradition it was the beginning of a new year. The Celtic year ended on the eve of Samhain (Hallowen) and began again on the day after. They considered it a Moon (month) of beginnings and endings and many still do.

The Japanese festival honouring the goddess of the kitchen honoured women who prepared the daily meals. Commonly called Kami, this goddess was important because by using the harvested food she protected and provided for the family.

The goddess Hecate had many celebrations throughout the year. November 16th was known as the Night of Hecate. Hecate is part of the most ancient form of the triple Moon goddess: Hecate, the Crone or Dark Moon; Artemis the Crescent Moon; and Selene, the Full Moon. Most of the worshipping of Hecate especially on this night, was performed at a three-way crossroad where food was left as an offering to her. She was known to rule the passages of life and transformation, birth and death. Her animals were the toad, the owl, the dog and the bat.

In Tibet, they celebrated the Feast of Lanterns, a winter festival of the shortest days of the Sun. Among the Incas, it was a time of the Ayamarca or Festival of the Dead.

Winter

'O Winter! bar thine adamantine doors:
The north is thine; there hast thou built thy dark
Deep founded habitation. Shake not thy roofs,
Nor bend thy pillars with thine iron car.'

William Blake

The winter solstice marks the time of year when light begins to return as the Sun starts to move northward again. Throughout Europe on this day a Yule log was placed on the hearth where it glowed for the twelve nights of the holiday season. The log was kept in the house all year to offer protection to the home and its inhabitants from illness and adversity.

The Yule log was the counterpart of the midsummer bonfires held outdoors on the summer solstice to celebrate the shortest night of the year. It was also customary to place mistletoe around the Yule fire. Mistletoe grows on the oak tree and was sacred to the Druids, the priests of the pagan Celts. Among other attributes, mistletoe had the power, it was thought, to help women conceive! Another Celtic ritual celebrated the renewal of the Earth where green foliage was used as a symbol of revival. Branches of pine, cedar, and juniper were commonly used and brought a wonderful fragrance into the home. Red candles were lit to symbolise the fire and heat of the returning Sun as the days began to lengthen.

The Earth is actually closer to the Sun in January than in June by about three million miles. This is the reason the Sun's disc appears slightly larger in winter. The seasons occur because the Earth leans slightly on its axis like a spinning top frozen in one lopsided position. This planetary posture causes all the variety of our climate and all the drama and poetry of our seasons. The lopsided posture of the Earth determines how many hours and minutes of Sunlight each hemisphere receives. Solstice means 'standing still Sun'.

At the winter solstice the Earth's northern hemisphere is leaning farthest away from the Sun and daylight is shortest because the Sun is at its lowest arc in the sky, and lies directly overhead along the Tropic of Capricorn. The Tropic of Capricorn lies south of the equator at latitude 23 degrees 27 minutes. It is the southern boundary of the tropics and marks the farthest point south the

Sun can be seen directly overhead at noon. The Tropic of Cancer lies north of the equator at latitude 23 degrees 27 minutes. It is the northern boundary of the tropics and marks the farthest point north the Sun can be seen directly overhead at noon. Their names originate from the signs of the zodiac: Capricorn and Cancer. However, the zodiac constellations no longer coincide with the original positions so perhaps we should update their names: the Tropic of Sagittarius and the Tropic of Gemini respectively.

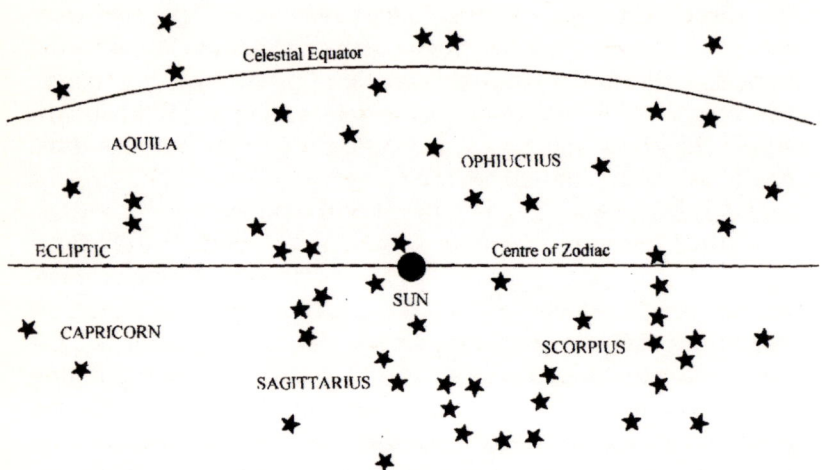

Fig 11 WINTER SOLSTICE The Sun no longer resides in the constellation of Capricorn at the winter solstice (Tropic of Capricorn) but in the constellation of Sagittarius.

When I can, I celebrate the winter solstice not with my friends and colleagues from the science world but with a community of New Age followers: environmentalists, pagans, Christians and people from across the globe. I travel with my family, including Red, to a New Age community settlement on the edge of the Lancashire moors between Pendle Hill and the Yorkshire moors. The winter moorland is bleak, cold, wuthering, dormant and yet magnificent and pagan. When I walk over the moors with Red, a wild mood often takes hold. It is as though I have been here before on the heath in a past life and I feel at home. Maybe I have a lost memory, a bio-ancestral connection or perhaps I am hearing the voice of the wind speaking to me over the centuries. Maybe I am simply beguiled by nature and my imagination. I don't know. It does not matter.

On the eve of midwinter as the Sun sets and darkness descends everyone at the settlement gathers around a bonfire to begin the celebration, and we are all excited like little children. Someone makes a speech and the bonfire is lit. It is not a massive bonfire but is big enough and is kept burning until dawn. Bonfires have always been a focal point at festivals and there are many endearing qualities of a good bonfire. They provide light on a dark night and have an element of drama. Their flickering colours, smoke, and noise provide excitement and warmth if the night is cold. They provide free heat for cooking and are a centre point for activities such as dancing, games and most importantly, eating. Bonfires consume wood, rubbish and moorland waste. Generally, anything that burns can be used and a bonfire cleans up all the deadwood and waste of the community.

The night is intensely dark. The light from the bonfire is not a harsh dazzling light and does not interfere with stargazing. Firelight is mostly at the red end of the spectrum anyway. The sky is clear and all the stars in heaven are shining. Throughout the night, we gaze up and marvel at the universe overhead pointing at satellites and rogue meteors as they streak across the sky. We feast on food grown and prepared locally and baked or roasted on the bonfire. We drink home brewed ale and mulled wine. Occasionally we walk away from the fire to be alone but we are soon drawn back to the fire. Several people play guitars, mandolins, flutes, hand held drums, tin whistles and harmonicas, and we dance and laugh. The children also dance and laugh and all the while, we gaze at the stars in heaven.

Surjit, Prem and Naseem chant an Indian melody and pound their two-skinned amaru drums, shaped like hourglasses and fitted with pellets that strike the skins when the drums are twirled. The rhythm and the beat of the drums are almost shamanic and we drift into a state of high consciousness. We feel disembodied and float among the star fields in heaven but we are aware of the flickering of the fire and the beating of the drums. As the night turns we sing old protest songs, 'We Shall Overcome' made popular by Joan Baez (originally a gospel song whose melody dates back to before the American Civil War). We sing songs from childhood, hymns, and we talk about the old days and it is wonderful. The first glimmer of pre-dawn twilight appears above the northeastern horizon and our little tribe observes the Sun rise on midwinter's morning, the way our forebears did, so long ago. The Earth, the sky and our little group all in harmony and synchronisation with the rhythm of life and the rhythm of the cosmos.

Clear Sky

The sky is clear and the stars are bright. Ursa Minor is three quarters way around from its starting position in March. The zodiac constellations of Gemini, Taurus, Aries, Aquarius and Capricorn can be seen. The sky is dark for a full fourteen hours and the Milky Way is clearly visible. The nights can be cold but Red and I are keen to be out. Indeed, Red is often straining at the leash to see his favourite constellation, Canis Minor, and his favourite star of course is Sirius the Dog Star, the brightest star in the sky!

Yule

Our Celtic ancestors celebrated Christmas as 'Yule' a few days before December 25th, and followed many of the traditional customs we associate with Christmas today: they decorated trees, sang carols, gave presents, burned the Yule log and kissed under the mistletoe. Their 'Nativity set' too had three central characters: Mother Nature, Father Time and the Sun god. The season we call 'Christmas' has always been more pagan than Christian with associations of Nordic divination, Celtic fertility rites and Roman Mithraism.

Martin Luther and John Calvin loathed Christmas and would not celebrate it. In the New World Christmas was even outlawed. Indeed Christmas was made illegal in England in the seventeenth century when the Puritans held power. Markets were ordered to stay open and even the baking of fancy pies and plum pudding were banned. On December 25th all church doors were locked. America was much later recovering from the Puritan influence. In 1856 Christmas Day was still an ordinary work day in Boston and failure to report to work was grounds for dismissal. Classes were held in Boston public schools as late as 1870. The first state to declare Christmas a legal holiday was Alabama in 1836. The last was Oklahoma in 1890. The holiday was too closely associated with the birth of older pagan gods and heroes. Many, Oedipus, Hercules, Perseus, Jason, Apollo, Mithra, possessed a narrative of birth, death, and resurrection uncomfortably close to that of Christ, and pre-dated him by a thousand years.

The holiday is deeply rooted in the cycle of the year. The winter solstice celebrates the longest night and shortest day and is the birthday of the new Sun King. The Earth Goddess becomes the Great Earth Mother and once again gives birth. The Western Church were late in laying claim to it as the time of Christ's birth, and tried more than once to reject it. Originally, the Western Church agreed Mary bore the child Jesus on the 25th day but could not decide in which month. In 320 AD the Fathers in Rome agreed to make it December in an effort to align the Mithraic celebration of the Romans and the Yule celebrations of the Celts and Saxons.

There was never much pretence about the chosen date being historically accurate. Shepherds do not 'tend their flocks by night' in the pastures in the dead of winter. If one wishes to use the New Testament as historical evidence, this reference may point to some time in the spring as the time of Jesus' birth. The lambing season occurs in the spring and is the only time shepherds are likely to 'watch their flocks by night' to make sure the lambing goes well. Knowing this, the Eastern half of the Church continued to reject December 25th preferring a 'movable date' fixed by their astrologers according to the Moon.

Despite its shaky start, December 25th finally began to catch on. By 529 AD it had become a Roman civic holiday and all work or public business was prohibited by the Emperor Justinian. In 563 AD the Council of Braga forbade fasting on Christmas Day and four years later, the Council of Tours proclaimed the twelve days from December 25th to Epiphany as a sacred festive season. Christmas was not a single day but a period of twelve days from December 25th to January 6th, indeed, the Twelve Days of Christmas.

Establishing Christmas

The Christian version of the holiday spread no faster than Christianity itself. Christmas was not celebrated in Ireland until the late fifth century and not in England, Switzerland or Austria until the seventh century; not in Germany until the eighth century and not in the Slavic lands until the ninth and tenth centuries. These countries had their own mid-winter celebration of Yuletide. Pagans have been observing the season for thousands of years by bringing in the Yule log, wishing on it and lighting it from the remains of last year's log. Riddles were posed and answered; magic and rituals were practised; wild boars were sacrificed and consumed along with large quantities of alcohol. Corn dollies were carried from house to house while carolling; fertility rites were practised and divinations were cast for the coming spring. Many of these customs in an appropriately watered down form have entered the popular Christmas celebration.

Yule, from the Anglo-Saxon 'Yula', meaning 'wheel' of the year is usually celebrated on the actual winter solstice. It is a lesser Sabbat or low holiday and one of the four quarter days of the year. Formerly, the Yule log (from an ash tree) had been the centre of the celebration and once lighted on the eve of the solstice, had to be kept burning for twelve hours for good luck. It should be lit on the first try. Later, the Yule log was replaced by the Yule tree but instead of burning it, burning candles were placed on it. The claim that Martin Luther or St. Boniface invented the custom is incorrect.

The holly, the ivy and the mistletoe were important plants of the season, all symbolising fertility and everlasting life. Mistletoe was especially venerated by the Celtic Druids who cut it with a special sickle on the sixth night of the Moon and believed it to be an aphrodisiac. (Do not try eating it. Mistletoe is highly toxic.) The Yuletide menu in ancient times indicates the tables fairly groaned under the strain of food and drink. The most popular drink was the 'wassail cup' of ale, deriving its name from the Anglo-Saxon term 'waes hael', be whole or hale.

Mediaeval Christmas folklore is endless: a windy Christmas will bring good luck; a person born on Christmas Day can see the Little People; if one opens all the doors of the house at midnight all the evil spirits will depart; you will have one lucky month for each Christmas pudding you sample; the tree must be taken down by Twelfth Night or bad luck is sure to follow, a custom we follow to this day. 'If Christmas on a Sunday be, a windy winter we shall see;' 'Hours of Sun on Christmas Day, so many frosts in the month of May'. One can use the Twelve Days of Christmas to predict the weather for each of the twelve months of the coming year.

The tradition of Father Christmas or Santa Claus does not spring from the three wise men giving gifts to the Christ child. It is a mixture of winter solstice festivals. The custom of exchanging gifts harks back to the Roman Saturnalia and can be traced all the way back to ancient Egypt. Scandinavian countries believe the god Odin visited the Earth to reward good and punish evil. As Christianity spread, Odin was replaced by St. Nicholas who brought gifts for good children. St. Nicholas was the Bishop of Myra in Asia Minor, who was imprisoned by the Romans because of his beliefs.

In Holland, St. Nicholas or Sinterklaas was believed to live in Spain, where he kept a large red book recording the children's good and bad deeds. On December 6th, he arrived in Amsterdam by ship with gifts. He came ashore on a white horse accompanied by servants. During the night, St. Nicholas rode across Holland leaving gifts for good children. The children filled their wooden shoes with food for the horse. It is from this tale we acquired the Santa Claus myth.

Around 1860, American artist Thomas Net created our modern Santa with red robes a white beard and a bundle of toys. His drawings were based on the 1822 poem 'A Visit From Saint Nicholas' by Clement Clark Moore.

> T'was the night before Christmas, when all through the house
> Not a creature was stirring, not even a mouse;
> The stockings were hung by the chimney with care,
> In hopes that St. Nicholas soon would be there.
> The children were nestled all snug in their beds,
> While visions of sugarplums danced in their heads;...

Not until St. Nicholas passed through the catalyst of Moore's mind did the patron saint of childhood ride in a sleigh, have eight tiny reindeer or dress in furs. The New York Institution for the Blind where Moore sat on the board of managers was located on 34th Street and hence the origin of the title of the motion picture 'Miracle on 34th Street'. Christmas has been developed commercially since the Industrial Revolution and not only do many of our traditional 'Christmas' customs have roots in pagan celebrations but the very festival itself can be traced to pagan practices.

At this time during the sixteenth century it was customary for English husbands to give their wives gloves, or the money to purchase them. This was known as 'glove money'. Later the gift of metal pins, or the money to purchase them was introduced. Eventually 'pin money' came to mean small amounts of cash women were allowed to spend in any manner they pleased during the centuries they lacked economic freedom.

Across the Globe

Neolithic peoples were the first farmers and their lives were intimately tied to the seasons and the cycles of the heavens. The earliest markers of time found from these ancient peoples are notches carved into bone, counting the cycles of the Moon. Our impulse to hold on to these traditions is strong today because they are echoes of a past that extends many thousands of years farther than we ever before imagined. An utterly astounding array of ancient cultures built their greatest architecture, tombs, temples, cairns and sacred observatories so that they were aligned with the solstices and equinoxes.

Stonehenge is a perfect marker of both solstices. New Grange is a beautiful megalithic site in Ireland. This huge circular stone structure is estimated to be older than Stonehenge and the Egyptian pyramids. The megalith was built to receive a shaft of sunlight deep into its central chamber at dawn on the winter solstice. The light illuminates a stone basin beneath intricate carvings of spirals, eye shapes and solar discs. Not a great deal is known of how the builders of New Grange used it, but marking the solstice was obviously of immense spiritual importance to them. Maeshowe on the Orkney Islands, north of Scotland shares a similar trait, admitting the winter solstice setting Sun. It is hailed as one of the greatest architectural achievements of the prehistoric peoples of Scotland.

Hundreds of megalithic structures throughout Europe are oriented to the solstices and the equinoxes which must have influenced the Celts in ways not yet uncovered. Sacred sites in the Americas, Asia, Indonesia, and the Middle East also seem to understand the importance of these Sun facing seasonal turning points, in spite of the fact they were cultures that followed a Moon-based calendar.

Romania

Apples are an old feature of this season. Apple wassailing was the mediaeval winter festival custom of blessing the apple trees with song, dance, decoration and a drink of cider to ensure their fertility. This was once a solstice ritual linked to the themes of nature's rebirth and fertility. In Romania, there is a traditional Christmas confection called a turta. It is made of many layers of pastry dough, filled with melted honey and hemp seed. In this tradition, with the making of the cake, families enact a little ceremony to assure the fruitfulness of their orchard in spring. When the woman is in the midst of kneading the dough, she follows her partner into the wintry garden. The man goes from barren tree to tree, threatening to cut each one down. Each time, the woman urges that he spare the tree by saying: 'Oh no, I am sure this tree will be as heavy with fruit next spring as my fingers are with dough this day.'

The East

Winter solstice celebrations are also part of the cultural heritage of Pakistan and Tibet. In China, even though the calendar is based on the Moon, the day of winter solstice is called Dong Zhi, 'the arrival of winter'. The cold of winter made an excellent excuse for a feast, so that is how the Chinese observed it, with Ju Dong, 'doing the winter'. In Iran, there is the observance of Yalda, in which families kept vigil through the night and fires burned brightly to help the Sun battle against darkness.

Hanukkah, the Jewish Festival of Lights occurs around this time every year. It is related to other celebrations of the season and its placement at this time of the year is a calendrical coincidence since it is based on the lunar Hebrew calendar.

In Russia, there is a Christmas divination that involves candles. A girl would sit in a darkened room with two lighted candles and two mirrors positioned so that one reflects the candlelight into the other. The viewer would seek the seventh reflection and look until her future could be seen.

The early Germans built a stone altar to Hertha or Bertha, goddess of domesticity and the home, during winter solstice. With a fire of fir boughs stoked on the altar, Hertha was able to descend through the smoke and guide those who were wise in Saga lore to foretell the fortunes of those at the feast.

Europe

In Spain, there is an old custom from Roman days where the urn of fate is a large bowl containing slips of paper on which are written all the names of those at a family get-together. The slips of paper are drawn out two at a time. Those whose names are so joined are to be devoted friends for the year. There is often a little subterfuge to help matchmaking along.

In Scandinavia some families would place all their shoes together as this would cause them to live in harmony throughout the year. In many cultures, it is considered bad luck for a fire or a candle to go out on Christmas Day.

My family and I attend several Carol Services each Christmas. I do so enjoy singing and (I think) have a fine voice! For a time, I sang each Christmas with a Salvation Army choir. I never actually joined, I just tagged along and really loved standing on a street corner under the stars singing carols, accompanied by a brass band. They didn't seem to mind. I have many favourite hymns but I do tend to sing 'Oh little star of Bethlehem, How still we see thee lie' when in the bath. Red croons along too. Like myself, he also has a good singing voice. I say to Red 'Red if we practise hard, we could sing two-part harmony with you as bass'. If the entire world could sing together, what a wonderful place it would be.

Fig 12 ORION AND CANIS MINOR Orion is the most distinctive

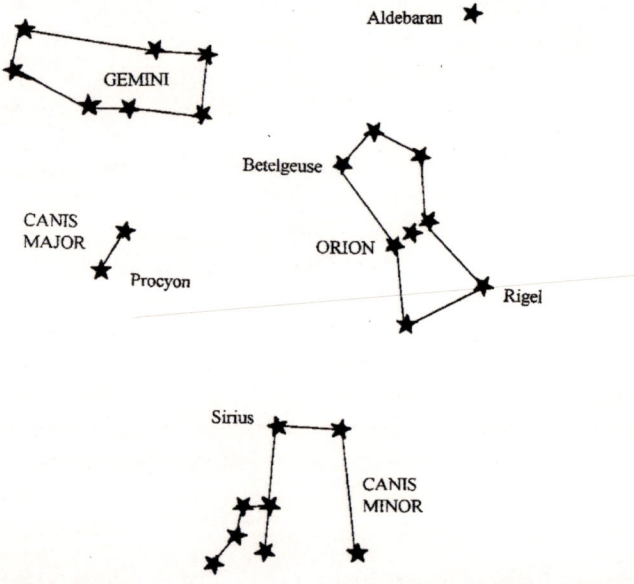

constellation in the sky. The central belt is easily identifiable. To the lower right lies the Blue Giant star Rigel and to the upper left hangs the Red Giant star Betelgeuse. Canis Minor is Red's favourite constellation and Sirius the Dog Star, his favourite star!

The chill of winter often keeps us indoors and away from the stars. Do not be scared of the cold, and do venture out under the stars. We are lucky the winter constellations offer more brightness per minute than at any other time of year. Look for the backbone of the winter stars. Orion is the best and most recognisable. Above the belt of Orion, to the right is the Red Giant star Betelgeuse and below the belt at the opposite side is the Blue Giant Rigel. The faint haze in the bottom centre is the famous nebula in Orion. The secret is to wrap up warm and do not think about the cold.

When visible, Jupiter is very bright, shining with a yellowish hue and like Mars, has a back loop in its orbit. Jupiter travels slowly across the sky and the Earth catches up easily so we have opposition at intervals of just over one year. It is therefore often visible all night long. With a good pair of binoculars, the four bright Galilean moons can be seen.

Comet Shoemaker-Levy 9, discovered by Eugene and Carolyn Shoemaker and David Levy, was first detected on a photograph March 1993. Through observations the comet's orbit was demonstrated to be around Jupiter and to have made a very close approach to Jupiter in July 1992. During this close approach, the unequal Jovian gravitational attractions on the comet's near and far sides broke the fragile object apart. The comet had as many as seventeen separate sub-nuclei strung out like pearls on a string. The disruption of a comet into multiple fragments is an unusual event. The capture of a comet into an orbit about Jupiter is even more unusual, and the collision of a large comet with a planet is an extraordinary, millennial event.

Why New Age?

One bitterly cold, clear night in January, Red and I had been observing from the Racecourse Park in Northampton until 10 pm. I had given an interview with Mark Whall on BBC Radio for the Eastern Counties earlier in the evening and before we set off home, we popped into the Racehorse Tavern. I ordered a Jack Daniels to warm me up. Red and I stood at the end of the bar, out of the way. A fierce looking young man, his arms covered in tattoos, with multiple facial piercings and a bright red, skin-head hair cut stood beside us at the bar.

I broke the ice: 'It's jolly cold out tonight' said I. 'Yeah?' growled the skinhead. 'You mate, you don't know what cold is, mate.' He continued with a mild cockney accent. 'I work on building sites, mate. I spend all day outside, mate so don't tell me about cold, mate.' 'It must be jolly cold working outside all day in this weather.' I replied. 'Yeah it is, mate. But it's worth it, mate. Ya see, I watch the Sun come up every mornin' and I see it go down at night, mate. The colours is amazin'. You ain't seen nothing like it, mate. It's worth freezin' just to see that, mate'.

I left the tavern rather astonished and I realised more than ever how everyone is moved by the realm of the sky. I had learned something that night. This intimidating-looking man who probably left full time education at sixteen years old and did not appear to be the sensitive, touchy, feely type was moved by the motion of the Sun and captivated by the colours of twilight. An old Tibetan riddle springs to mind:

A flag moves.
What is it that moves,
The flag, or the wind?
It is the Mind that moves.

Many people ask why I call myself a New Age Astronomer. I grew up in a small rural borough on the edge of the Lancashire moors and more or less experienced life as it had been lived for hundreds of years previously. Electricity had just come on line and televisions, telephones, refrigerators, computers; all modern technology lay in the immediate future. My grandmother lived in the 1880s. Her grandmother had direct contact with people who lived in the 1780s and much of the knowledge within our community had been handed down in an oral tradition. The community was rich in folklore. Local women, including my mother knew all about the magic of herbs and how each was influenced by the stars in heaven.

We visited the 'herb shop' regularly, an Aladdin's Cave of bubbling cauldrons, magic potions and sorcerer's spells. Herbs have served humankind since the dawn of time as food and in promoting health. Leaves, berries, bark, roots, seeds and flowers were ground, steamed and distilled. Poultices were macerated and chopped herbs placed directly on the skin and a hot, moist bandage applied as a cure for many ailments. I remember these remedies and the time, effort and magic associated with each potion. Our larder stocked everything: Dandelion, Burdock root, Chamomile, Cinnamon, Comfrey, Lavender, Ginger, Liquorice, Mustard, Hawthorne Berries, St John's Wort and Rosemary.

Modern pharmacological technology did not exist. Electronic technology did not exist and my direct experience of this has everything to do with my New Age approach to astronomy. My childhood included astrology, tealeaf reading, tarot, palmistry and a thousand other folk practices. One could see the night sky clearly as there was no light pollution. The stars and especially the Moon played an important part. Their motions and phases affected everything we did and their influence touched the essence of our soul.

I studied Physics and Astronomy at university, I have taught Physics at school, electronics at college and communication systems to university undergraduates. I know how things work, how the universe is constructed and yet this knowledge does not teach me my obligations to this planet and the cosmos. Everything on Earth is being continuously transformed because the Earth is alive. The Earth has a soul and we are all part of that soul. The Earth is working for us and there is only one Earth. The Earth is a great little planet and I love it. Hard scientific facts and the Science Education Movement do not instruct one in the skills of looking after this precious little gift. This is why I am a New Age scientist. I desire a thoughtful, harmonious, multi-disciplined or 'holistic' approach to the study of Science and Astronomy. I am a scientist but most of all, I am a man of the moors, of nature and of the Earth and Sky!

The West is a world of material plenty, high standards of health care and a diet of unimaginable variety, so why are stress, anxiety and depression responsible for the greatest suffering in all technological societies? More working days are lost and family life irrevocably disrupted by the despair of mental illness than by all other disorders put together. I will tell you why: uncertainty, lack of security and the inability of society, community and the individual to hold an opinion or have faith in any meaningful belief system have harvested a loss of self confidence and a loss of self direction and purpose. The extended family became the nuclear family and is now the proton family, soon to be the virtual family, detached, without roots and alone.

My childhood life ran like clockwork. Every action completed was a repetition of a previous action, performed with efficiency, on time and with the cosmic environment taken into account. Everything had a purpose. Family life mirrored nature and revolved around the patterns, rhythms, circles and cycles of daily rituals just as the patterns, rhythms, circles and cycles of nature revolved around the cosmos. Just knowing an event would happen at such a time and on such a date provided stability. The seasons came and passed, the phases of the Moon recurred and the Sun rose and set every day, and we were aware of these events. There was order in the universe and order in my home and all was well.

Hindsight tells me these patterns, rituals and cosmic connections were the most stabilising influence in my life. I didn't know it at the time but I think I do now. If we listen to our heart we would realise there is a big difference between knowing the path and walking the path. Today we all know the path we should follow, but many, to their detriment, are deterred from or are unable to walk it.

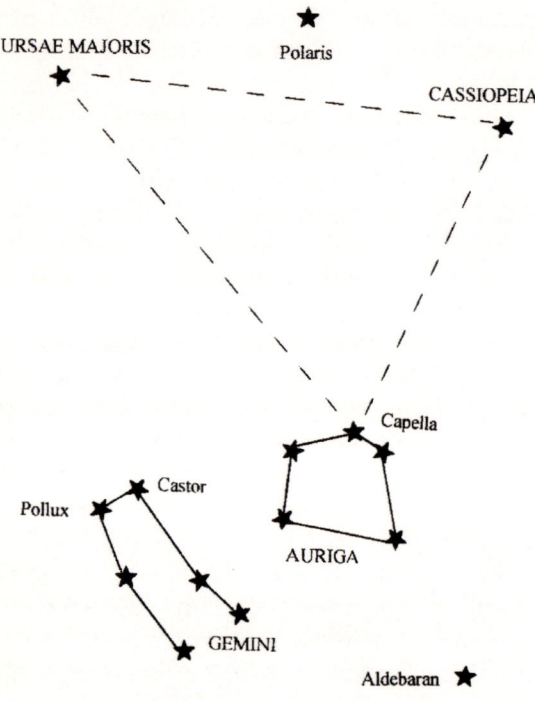

Fig 13 GEMINI Dark skies offer excellent views of the star constellations spanning the zodiac.

If you have been out stargazing you will have probably spent a lot of time staring at Orion, the Pleiades and Sirius. They are the most striking constellations. However, this is also a good time to observe Gemini, Taurus and Cancer.

The most distant planet known to the ancients was Saturn, planet of the rings. Saturn is undoubtedly the most beautiful planet in the solar system if viewed through a telescope, and the rings are visible. Saturn moves very slowly against the stellar background and is not as bright as Jupiter but still easy to pick out among the background stars. Saturn also appears to move backwards in the sky as the Earth approaches and races past it.

Imbolc

It seems quite possible the holiday of Candlemas should be considered the beginning of spring. The days are noticeably lighter and the tenuous beginnings of little buds, flowers and leaves are apparent. It is the perfect time for a Festival of Lights. 'Candlemas' is the Christianised name for the older pagan holiday of Imbolc or Oimelc. 'Imbolc' means 'in the belly' of the Mother. 'Oimelc' means 'milk of ewes' for February is the beginning of the lambing season.

The holiday is also called 'Brigit's Day' in honour of the Irish goddess Brigit. At her shrine, followers kept an eternal flame burning in her honour. She was considered a goddess of fire, patroness of smith crafts, poetry and healing, especially the healing touch of midwifery. This tripartite symbolism occasionally expressed itself by saying Brigit had two sisters, also named Brigit. Another form of the name Brigit is Bride and it is she who bestows her special patronage on a woman about to be married, the woman being called 'bride' in her honour.

The Church could not easily abandon the great goddess of Ireland and so they canonised her as Saint Brigit. Brigit's holiday was chiefly marked by the kindling of sacred fires since she symbolised the fire of birth and healing, the fire of the forge and the fire of poetic inspiration. The Church quickly confiscated this symbolism too, using Candlemas as the day to bless all the church candles that would be used for the coming liturgical year. Catholics will be reminded the following day, St. Blaise's Day which is celebrated by using the newly blessed candles to bless the throats of parishioners, keeping them from colds, flu and sore throats.

The Western Church also called it the Feast of the Purification of the Blessed Virgin Mary. The symbol of the Purification may seem a little obscure but it is connected with the old custom of 'churching women'. Women were considered impure for six weeks after giving birth. Since Mary gave birth at the winter solstice she would not be purified until February 2nd. In pagan symbolism, this may be re-translated as the Great Mother once again becoming the Young Maiden Goddess. This holiday is connected to weather mythology and as an old British rhyme reminds us 'If Candlemas Day be bright and clear, there'll be two winters in the year.'

Candlemas may be celebrated on an alternative astrological date determined by the Sun reaching fifteen degrees in Aquarius on the fixed zodiac. This same displacement is evident in the Eastern Orthodox Church. Their habit of celebrating the birth of Jesus on January 6th, with a similar post dated shift in the six-week period that follows, puts the Feast of the Purification of Mary on February 14th.

Valentine

Another holiday, which ties in with this astrological date is Valentine's Day, February 14th. Indeed, the Church has always found it rather difficult to explain this nebulous saint's connection to the secular pleasures of flirtation and courtly love. Candlemas may then be seen astrologically as the pagan version of Valentine's Day, with a de-emphasis of 'hearts and flowers' and an appropriate re-emphasis of pagan carnal frivolity. This also re-aligns the holiday with the ancient Roman Lupercalia, a fertility festival held at this time in which the priests of Pan ran through the streets of Rome whacking young women with goat skin thongs to make them fertile.

One folk custom still practised in many countries is to place a lighted candle in each and every window of the house beginning at Sunset on Candlemas Eve (February 1st), allowing them to continue burning until Sunrise. I stopped this practice as one year, I placed a burning candle too near the curtains which set ablaze after an hour. Red came to the rescue by alerting me but the curtains were ruined. I said to Red 'Red, you are a life saver'. Red bowed gracefully. He is such a modest dog!

Other customs of the holiday include weaving 'Brigit's cross', a corn dolly or knot of straw or wheat to hang around the house for protection, performing rites of spiritual cleansing and purification, making 'Brigit's beds' to ensure fertility of mind, spirit and body if desired. This Pagan Festival of Lights, dedicated to the young Maiden Goddess is one of the most delightful and dreamy of the year. Crowns of Light, similar to those worn on St. Lucy's Day in Scandinavian countries were worn!

Lunar Myths

The Irish say never cut your hair, begin a journey, move into a new house, start a business on a Friday especially if a New or Full Moon falls on a Friday. The name Mount St. Helens means 'Moon Mountain'. The Word 'create' has the same genesis as the word 'crescent'. The Egyptians said the Dark Moon and the Full Moon were the two eyes of Horus. The horseshoe is a symbol of the lunar crescent. Certain ancient British coins had the horse and the crescent on them. For the horseshoe and the crescent Moon to be lucky and to hold the luck, the horns must be turned upwards.

The natives of Madagascar call their isle the Island of the Moon. To aim at the Moon means to be very ambitious, to set your sights extremely high. The eastern branches of the Eskimo clans say their people came from the Moon to Earth.

To wish on the Moon in order to see a specific person soon, one must say while looking at the Moon: 'I see the Moon, The Moon sees me. The Moon sees (name of the person) who I want to see.' If a New Moon falls on a Saturday there would be twenty days of wind and rain. In prophesying marriage, one must look at the first Moon of the New Year through a silk handkerchief. The number of Moons showing through it represents the number of months, Moons of single life. A snowy February brings a good spring while a mild month means stormy weather ahead.

In Cornwall, if a boy was born during a waning Moon they said the next birth would be a girl. In Wales if you moved from one house to another during the Crescent Moon you would have more than enough prosperity in your life. When anyone spoke of Mountains of the Moon it simply meant White Mountains. The Arabs called white horses 'Moon coloured'. Mt. Sinai was originally named after the Chaldean Moon god Sinn which would make it another Moon Mountain. In Italy they say if the Moon changes on a Sunday there will be a flood before the month is out.

December Moon

December Moon names are: Cold Moon, Oak Moon, and Winter Moon. December was the tenth month on the old Roman calendar, the month containing the carefree Saturnalia. The Franks called it Heilagmanoth or Holy Month because of its large number of sacred festivals.

On the old Tibetan calendar December 1st was the beginning of a new year. The ancient Mayan goddess Ixchel is still honoured in southern Mexico with processions and rituals that bless boats and fields. Her worship at one time extended through southern Mexico, the Yucatan Peninsula as far as El Salvador.

The winter solstice was celebrated and it was the time when virgin mothers give birth to sacred sons: Rhiannon to Pryderi, Isis to Horus, and Demeter to Persephone. The birth of Horus was celebrated about December 23rd, shortly after the winter solstice and the time of Osiris's final entombment. At this time of the year, Isis and Nephthys were said to have circled the shrine of Osiris seven times symbolising their mourning and searching for his scattered body parts. In Japan it was the time when the hiding Sun goddess Amaterasu came out of her cave.

January Moon

January Moon names are: Wolf Moon, Quiet Moon, Snow Moon, Cold Moon, Chaste Moon. The word January comes from the Roman name for this month and was named after the god Janus who had two faces. This deity ruled over beginnings and endings, the past and the future. Since January is the first month of a new year it is appropriately connected with the god Janus. It is an excellent time to work on putting aside the old and the outdated in one's life and making plans for new and better conditions.

The Chinese use this concept in celebrating their New Year which occurs on the first day of the New Moon when the Sun is in Aquarius. They considered this celebration a time for settling debts, honouring ancestors and having family reunions. They carry paper images of dragons through the streets and set off fireworks to chase away evil entities and misfortune.

February Moon

February Moon names are: Ice Moon, Storm Moon, Horning Moon, Hunger Moon, Wild Moon, Winter Moon. Some say the name of the month of February comes from the Roman goddess Februa who was also known as Juno Februa. Others say the name came from the god Februus who was later identified with the Roman Pluto or Dis.

The month of February is mostly a month of ice in many parts of the northern hemisphere, though not so much in the British

Isles. It is a dormant time when all activity and life appears to be hidden below the surface. In both Celtic and Roman cultures it was a time of spiritual purification and initiation. Tibet celebrated the conception of Buddha and the Feast of Flowers at this time of year.

Kuan Yin, the great goddess of the Oriental people has been known to offer her aid primarily to women and girls, but there is no reason why men cannot honour her and ask for her help. She is said to guide lost travellers, protect people from attack by humans or animals, bless a family with children and heal. She is called the Compassionate and is revered for her wisdom and love. Oriental women offered oranges and spices before her statue.

Part Two

The Blue Horizon: Ancient Cosmic Wheel

The Atomic Age began at exactly 05:30 Mountain War Time on the morning of July 15th 1945 on a stretch of semi-desert land about five miles from Alamogordo, New Mexico.

'... now I am become Death, the destroyer of worlds ...'

Robert Oppenheimer
Supervising Scientist of the Manhattan
(Atom Bomb) Project

If the radiance of a thousand Suns
Were to burst at once into the sky
That would be like the splendour of the Mighty one
I am become Death,
The shatterer of Worlds.

Original quote—*Bhagavad-Gita*

Roots

When the first human journeyed beyond the communication of objective experience and expressed a subjective experience we saw the birth of a new world, the world of ideas. All cultures are the result of this symbiosis: objective experience and subjective conception. Every culture has within it residual traces of this two-fold conscious embryo stretching back all the way to its inception: the roots of archetypal memories, beliefs and traditions. The festivals we celebrate today are echoes from a pre-recorded past. Our cultural beliefs and practices are based upon the template of stars in the sky and the patterns, rhythms, circles and cycles contained within the movement of heaven and Earth.

The prodigious development of objective science over the past four centuries has forced society to make a radical reappraisal of its twin consciousness: objectivity and subjectivity. The concept of subjective thought rooted in our consciousness for tens of thousands of years is today viewed by mainstream science as unworthy. Society also unconsciously adheres to this point of view and as a consequence society has become a slave to the tyranny of reason and its pervasive influence. The science-dominated society has brought many material benefits, yet it has disconnected humankind from nature and from their essence. This subtle dissociation has led to an imbalance and a disharmony of mind, body and spirit energy.

Myth

Society operates on two levels: the mind and ideas and the world of external accomplishment. The value of an idea in terms of its external manifestation depends upon the change it brings to the behaviour or survival of the culture that adopts it. The society adopting an idea which increases survival, flourishes as a result of the idea, which further promotes the idea. The spreading power of an idea depends upon pre-existing structures of the mind, among them, ideas already implanted by culture. The ideas having the highest invading potential are those that give society an assured future. For hundreds of thousands of years the survival strategy of the individual was identical to that of the tribe to which they belonged. The tribe could only survive and defend itself through union. Out of this union arose the subjective power of the laws that organise and guarantee human bonding both on an individual and social scale.

The development of myths and religions, and the construction of vast philosophical systems provided a cultural heritage. But a cultural heritage would not alone have been strong enough to hold up the social structure. The heritage needed and acquired a cosmic connection, a supernatural force, a power that could control destiny and provide something essential to the mind: a spiritual refuge. Astrological and animist beliefs are invariably at the base of all social structures. The variety of myths, religions and philosophical ideologies appear to be diverse but essentially all have the same basic ingredients: Heaven and Earth, mind, body and spirit.

In the course of four centuries, science has taken its place in society but not in the hearts of its members. Modern societies are built upon the miracle of science, engineering and technology. To this miracle, they owe their wealth, their power and the assurance of more wealth and more power tomorrow. The twentieth century promised science would lead to a vast blossoming for humankind, whereas we see before us today the flames of the inferno. Each year, thousands of species tumble into extinction, mechanised warfare on a scale unimaginable creates hunger, disease, poverty, homelessness and tens of millions of refugees.

Our craving for material comfort is depleting the ozone layer and is responsible for atmospheric pollution which in turn irradiates the Earth and produces global warming. The Earth's oceans are contaminated and over-fished, once fertile land is turning to desert, nuclear fission threatens our existence and genetic engineering's crowning glory 'the terminator gene' is on the horizon. We are told the Human Genome Project will eventually lead to the discovery of every gene responsible for every human ailment, disorder and disease. The Human Genome Project will not find the most important gene of all, because there are no genes for the soul or the spirit. However one defines the soul or the spirit it will not be discovered by the autocracy of reason. Only by searching intuitively within ourselves will we find our soul.

Fifty years ago, scientists described the world of the future, a world where nuclear power would generate electricity so cheaply and safely there would be no need to install meters. Today, the nuclear industry is in tatters. Nuclear power is expensive and dangerous. It will take millions of years for hazardous radioactive waste material to become safe. Today, scientists of the same ilk tell of a world where genetically modified structures will feed, clothe and heal humanity safely and cheaply. But we already know the terrible truth. Scientists provide Third World countries with seed that does not reproduce and so Third World countries become locked into a system of dependency and increasing debt.

Genetically modified structures are designed to cross the species barrier and once unleashed, there is no way of retrieving them. The so-called terminator gene may cross the species barrier and mix with grass, trees and flowers? If this occurs eventually grass, trees and flowers will be unable to pollinate and therefore reproduce. Could we be responsible for a world barren of all plant life? The terminator gene may cross the species barrier with ourselves. The gene will be present in the food we eat. The terminator gene will be inside us! No one can be against adding vitamin A to rice to make it more nutritious, but let us not blindly blunder into genetic oblivion!

Detachment

Science has detached us from our roots and we are floating in the ether without protection and with no host values on which to attach ourselves. The spreading power of an idea depends upon pre-existing structures of the mind, among them ideas already implanted by culture. There were no pre-existing structures of the mind, no ideas already implanted in our culture when science erupted into being. At least, these pre-existing mind patterns were regarded by scientists as worthless, as harmful clutter from which the mind needed to be freed, to make way for pure, objective reason.

Science demolishes all in its wake, it is relentless, remorseless, uncaring, unfeeling, and indifferent to our suffering and it will not stop. Science will continue to advance because once unleashed that is all it does. That is all science can do, and we have been so mesmerised by its capacity we have failed to keep it in check. We have marvelled at its magnificence, at our own magnificence, but we have lost our soul in the process.

Science is concerned only with brute facts: observing, weighing, measuring, and testing without further questions being asked. Science is value free. Science does not know right from wrong and it needs protecting against itself. Science is not the only source of truth and it is altogether unsatisfactory for scientists to suggest science is the only way of understanding the world. Science dominates modern societies but in the process of doing so, we have become its prey and must now more than ever, provide a counterweight to science.

Our inner experience, our values, our morality and our responsibility are undermined because science or rather the scientists who engage in science believe they know the truth. Science's authoritarianism, especially within the Science Education Movement leads to a closed view of the world and if we allow this to continue, the very opposite of what Science Education is trying to achieve, occurs. Their ideology becomes worse than any evil they started out to combat. It starts quietly, undetected and ends with the most brutal destruction of all that is human! Science should be triumphant, and would be if only scientists acknowledged the limitations of science.

Truth

There are many kinds of truth beyond the brute facts of the world. Science denies the value of subjective experience. An encyclopaedia contains a large number of correct statements which are based on knowledge, on the truth. However, we do not consult an encyclopaedia to discover the kind of truth by which we wish to live our lives. Only the subjective method, a method used by humankind for tens of thousands of years can reveal a truth, which, in contrast to factual information, can become a personal experience and thereby have a deep influence upon what we do and believe. To discover the truth by which we wish to live our lives, we must start from personal experience and base our ideas on it, not vice versa.

The rise of techno-paganism is a natural consequence of the inability of scientists to allow space for any moral leadership or spiritual direction for technological societies to follow. The irrationality of existence must be faced if we are to live a meaningful, life however irrational it becomes. The visionary, William Blake, (Urizen) does not oppose reason, but he does oppose its tyranny over other human faculties, warning it will destroy the world unless the wholesome spirit awakens. How true his warning today. Soren Kierkegaard tells us reasonable demonstrations are irrelevant in the context of the human spirit. It is possible to choose in the absence of all knowledge or evidence because to choose is part of what it is to be human.

Intuition and reason belong together side by side. They are equal partners. Intuition and reason occupy equal physical space within our brain, the two hemispheres: left brain and right brain. Objectivity and subjectivity influenced the ancient world and through these two methods, discovered their first discipline: astrology. All other wisdom: astronomy, mathematics, meteorology, medicine, philosophy, etc. stem from and were subordinate to the first discipline. In order to understand the ancients we are forced to accept astrology in its widest sense and to accept it was an important force in historic times. To understand the present we need to examine our roots reasonably and intuitively and not evaluate ancient cultures by modern standards and assign motives to historic events in accordance with current principles. Ancient cultures, like modern cultures cannot be understood by reason alone.

The Signs of the Zodiac

The origin of the signs of the zodiac is not a great mystery. Their creation lies in our festival quarter days and the endless patterns, rhythms, circles and cycles of nature. The Sun travels across the sky along a path known as the ecliptic. The zodiac is the narrow band of sky laying either side of the ecliptic and along which travel the Moon and planets. The star constellations lying within the band of the zodiac make the signs of the zodiac. The word zodiac stems from the Roman 'zodiacus' which is derived from the Greek word 'zodiakos' and literally means circle of animals. The signs of the zodiac are based on the turning of the seasons and the astro-psychological meaning behind each zodiac figure or constellation is also based on the turning of the seasons.

The zodiac starts on the day of the spring equinox, a day acknowledged as special by Megalithic and Mediterranean peoples. The ancient Celts used a thirteen zodiac lunar calendar based on the cycle of the Moon. The modern signs of the zodiac, the ones we are familiar with originate from the Middle East and the Mediterranean region and can be traced back 3000 years to Sumeria and Babylon. This early zodiac used eighteen signs. The twelve Sun sign zodiac appeared in Babylon and ancient Greece around 500 BC. Not all of the same animals were used and not always in the same time periods, as we know them today.

The star constellation directly behind the rising Sun on the day of the spring equinox was Aries. Throughout the year the Sun travelled through the different star constellations of the zodiac and therefore each 'month' is assigned a sign of the zodiac. From March 21st to April 20th the Sun travelled through the Constellation Aries, or Aries the Ram. Symbolically, spring is the cycle of growth in nature and many of the qualities of the season were introjected within the Aries astro-personality. The four principal zodiac signs are the Cardinal (fundamental) signs which mark the frame of reference for the zodiac and explain why the signs were oriented to the equinox and solstice points. The division of the four seasons are:

1st day of Spring: Aries
1st day of Summer: Cancer
1st day of Autumn: Libra
1st day of Winter: Capricorn

The twelve zodiac signs are based on events associated with the seasons. The symbolic animals and figures within the star constellations possess characteristics relevant to the seasons on Earth: agriculture, events in nature, increasing or decreasing light, temperature, humidity, all of which have distinct effects on human and animal behaviour and their environment. Different cultures saw different animals in the sky: the northern constellation called Ursa Major or the Big Dipper was seen as The Great Bear by the ancient Greeks, as a Bull and Hippopotamus in ancient Egypt, as a Wagon in Mediaeval Europe, as a Seated Bureaucrat in ancient China and as a Plough in England. My wife calls it the Saucepan!

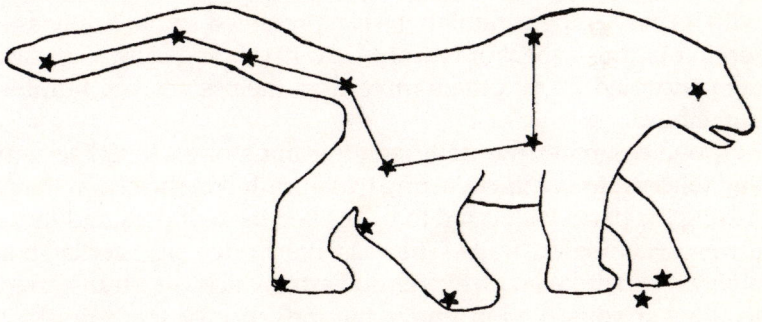

Fig 14 URSA MAJOR The Great Bear of the ancient Greeks is composed of seven bright stars. My wife calls it the Saucepan!

China, India, Africa, Australasia and the Americas used completely different animals and figures to represent beings and objects superimposed onto the star constellations. These cultures also developed independently and in isolation from one another and yet the inspiration to picture animals and figures in the sky, including the zodiac must have derived from a common or universal source. Their creative, spiritual energy flowed from that reservoir of thought hidden within the collective unconscious. The pictures the ancients saw were not really in the night sky. The animals and figures our ancestors traced onto the sky were extensions of their perception of reality. The pictures existed only within their minds. They were symbolically placed on the template of the heavens to reinforce seasonal conditions and life experienced on Earth. The stars, which form the constellations in the sky, are not really connected and are many light years from one another. The constellation stars appear connected when observed from Earth because our line of sight view is two-dimensional.

The star constellations and signs of the zodiac have no resemblance to any animals or any other figures. It is almost impossible to look at the constellation of Leo and be able to see the outline of a lion. Try it! I have tried it many times and it is difficult to trace anything other than simple patterns, a 'W', a cross or a single line. Each original zodiac sign is a symbol of a deeper meaning with a seasonal relevance. For example, the star constellation of Aries and its astro-psychological interpretation has everything to do with the Earth's seasonal character of spring. Aries, the Ram, just like spring is impulsive and down to earth. The sign of Virgo with its harvesting connotations is represented symbolically as a virgin holding a sheaf of wheat. Astro-psychologically, Virgoans are concerned about others more than themselves, are humble and ethical.

If one compares the traditional meaning of each zodiac sign and relates it to events occurring in nature and in society on Earth during the period allocated to it, one begins to understand these astro-psychological traits. The seasonal twelve sign zodiac has always been linked with events on Earth, which were transferred to the star constellation under the influence of the Sun. As a result, the signs of the zodiac, the constellations in the sky became inextricably linked with events on Earth. The seasonal conditions were metamorphosed to the figure traits of the constellations represented. The process worked in both directions: the season's characteristics were transferred to the appropriate sign of the zodiac and the sign of the zodiac bestowed the season with its poetry. The star constellations were a registered image of the seasonal changes projected onto the heavenly template over 2000 years ago.

The spring equinox is the calibration point of the zodiac and the shifting of the constellations caused by the Earth's precession, a wobble of the Earth's polar axis, has moved the original signs of the zodiac out of phase. The result is the constellation of Aries has shifted by almost one full sign so that now, Pisces is positioned behind the Sun during that time of year. Also there are now thirteen signs of the zodiac. Many astronomers use the precession to discredit astrological zodiac signs. Mainstream astronomers have failed to understand the nature of the zodiac signs and their association with the seasonal effects on humans, animals and nature. The star signs or constellations were a carbon copy of the seasons on Earth. To understand the astro-psychological zodiac traits we must concentrate on their origins of 2000 years ago.

Origin of meanings for the Signs of the zodiac

The animals and figures allocated to the twelve zodiac signs are based on the seasonal environment rather than any patterns in the star constellations. The traditional meanings of each sign were based on events in nature and society that occurred during the period allotted to each sign. These events in nature became first impressions for all born at such times. Autumn is my favourite season, maybe because I was born in autumn. Impressions became etched permanently not only in the individual psyche but on the collective unconscious too. Perhaps the zodiac is inside each one of us.

Spring

> The Constellation Aries or Aries the Ram:
> March 21st to April 20th

Seasonal characteristics: It is the time of the spring equinox and daylight is longer than darkness providing more heat. Buds and seeds sprout suddenly and life begins. The old cycle of growth ends and a new one begins. Animals come out of hibernation, birds return while barn doors open and farmers prepare for work.

Personal characteristics: Impulsive, active, rash, bold, impatient, restless, ambitious, exploitative, desirous of starting new things, pioneering, loving adventure, daring, challenging, tough, outgoing, headstrong, optimistic, cheerful.

> The Constellation Taurus or Taurus the Bull:
> April 21st to May 22nd

Seasonal characteristics: The ground heats up, the soil softens and roots develop. There is action in the soil and farmers plough the fields and plant crops. Gardeners prepare soil beds while farmers examine the roots of seedlings and study stem forms. Home foundations are constructed and nature becomes green in colour. Many flowers appear and there is a sense of beauty in nature.

Personal characteristics: Practical, down to earth, solid, firm, stable, fixed in position, possessive, having sound values, admiring strength, steady, reliable, liking objects of dependability such as gold, silver, gems, precious metals, money, bonds; security conscious, supportive, needing structure, traditional, loving voluptuous forms, appreciative of nature, beauty, art and all things of lasting value.

> The Constellation Gemini or Gemini the Twins:
> May 22nd to June 23rd.

Seasonal characteristics : There is action in the air as small branches and leaves expand in vast quantity. Young crops demand attention and busy schedules require bodily movement. Short distance trips and many relationships are renewed or formed. Marriage, excitement and outdoor activities occur. Insects and birds fill the air.

Personal characteristics: Communicative, talkative, bookish, learning, loving to travel, restless, scatty, expressive, active, witty, wanting constant change, adaptable, changeable, flexible, fickle, having many ideas and starting many things, liking to plan, friendly, flirtatious, knowledgeable, having an answer for everything.

Summer

> The Constellation Cancer or Cancer the Crab:
> June 24th to July 22nd.

Seasonal characteristics : The Sun is at its highest declination in sky. The summer solstice arrives bringing sunlight and heat. Animals seek shelter and humans get cranky, irritable and stressed from high temperatures. The crops and humans require much water and humans seek shelter from the heat. Children are at home and parents play with children.

Personal characteristics: Sheltering, protective, nurturing, moody, sentimental, highly strung, snappy, sensitive, cranky, temperamental, compassionate, generous, warm, family-oriented, property-minded, having a tough shell with soft interior, patronising, condescending, acting older than one's age.

The Constellation Leo or Leo the Lion:
July 23rd to August 22nd.

Seasonal characteristics : There is much sunshine, blue skies and warm breezes. Farmers feel confident as crops reach maturity and they speculate on how much the crop will bring at the market. It is an ideal time for relaxation, fun, play and entertainment. Plants are in fertility, and it is time for romance and preparation of creative methods for harvesting crops.

Personal characteristics: Regal sense of being born at the best time of the year, having a sense of self importance, proud, superior, liking to dictate to others, arrogant, self-centred, a liking to be centre of attention, fun-loving, playful, pouting, throwing fits, spoiled, dramatic, theatrical, vain, outgoing, energetic, creative, superficial.

The Constellation Virgo or Virgo the Virgin:
August 23rd to September 22nd.

Seasonal characteristics: The daylight decreases, the temperature gets cooler and the crops are harvested. All able hands are in the fields and picking the ripe crops. A critical eyesight and judgment for selecting ripest fruits is required when collecting. Sorting, packing and hard work can cause health problems.

Personal characteristics: Critical, analytical, finicky, liking to collect, hard working, good at details, preferring intricate ornamental art, earthy, practical, cooperative, devoted, meticulous, careful, sharp-eyed, good at sorting and arranging, loving to eat, tending to be a workaholic, concerned about others more than one-self, humble, ethical, self-denying in a materialistic sense.

Autumn

The Constellation Libra or Libra the Scales:
September 23rd to October 22nd.

Seasonal characteristics: It is the time of the autumn equinox when darkness increases and the first frost bites. Packaged crops are weighed on the scales at market and goods are evaluated. The value of goods is determined, business partnerships are forged and retail sales made. People exercise the art of bargaining and diplomacy. Socialising accompanies business deals and romance mixes with business.

Personal characteristics: Social, graceful, diplomatic, refined, easy-going, friendly, evaluating, objective, hesitant, indecisive, loving to make deals, appreciative of balance, loving justice, respectful of fair play, cool in attitude, enjoying the good life, flirtatious, loving to collect art works and valuables.

The Constellation Scorpio or Scorpio the Scorpion: October 22nd to November 22nd

Seasonal characteristics: There is death in nature while weather is cold, wet and overcast. A gloomy feeling begins and preparations are made for winter. All work is done in a hurry and emotions run high. Resources are shared and people help others to finish outdoor jobs. Social events increase indoors, and sudden late marriages take place as plants drop their seeds.

Personal characteristics: Emotionally intense, secretive, powerful, magnetic, desperate, mysterious, vindictive, resentful, overbearing, controlling, extremely sociable or withdrawn, hyper active or unusually calm, having a mind for lucrative business, exploitative, excitable, resourceful, materialistic, envious, jealous, imaginative, eccentric.

The Constellation Sagittarius or Sagittarius the Archer: November 23rd to December 22nd.

Seasonal characteristics : The darkness increases and all attention is focused on the festivities for the end of the year. The atmosphere is jovial; parties and family re-unions are planned. Gifts are bought and everything is done in a frenzied and religious way. People travel long distances to experience foreign culture and knowledge is gained.

Personal characteristics: Cheerful, optimistic, jovial, sociable, elitist, noble, aristocratic, sophisticated, knowledgeable, smug, daring, exploitative, adventurous, almost reckless, spiritually enlightened, righteous, moralistic, condescending, patronising, ceremonious, superior.

Winter

The Constellation Capricorn or Capricorn the Goat:
December 23rd to January 21st.

Seasonal characteristics: The winter solstice arrives and darkness falls. It is time to conserve energy and food. There is a need for good management of resources so food lasts for animals and humans. There is a need for rules and control. The role for authority figures has an emphasis on responsibility and social duties. (Food was not imported and supermarkets did not exist.)

Personal characteristics: Authoritative, ambitious, duty-conscious, responsible, sociable, conservative, serious, conformist, administrative, controlling, disciplined, organised, systematic, methodical, careful, persevering, traditional, reserved, austere, persistent, stubborn, strong-willed, devoted, reliable.

The Constellation Aquarius or Aquarius the Water bearer:
January 21st to February 20th.

Seasonal characteristics : The light and temperature increases and there is a sense of optimism in the air. There is a natural tendency to look forward to the New Year and new ideas. Farmers think of how to improve the next crop yield and various plans and projects are considered. The harshest weather at this time forces people to react with determination and to have innovative survival strategies.

Personal characteristics: Sociable, friendly, intellectual, optimistic, liberal, reformist, political, freedom-loving, independent, different, unconventional, eccentric, cheerful, humorous, occasionally pessimistic, conservative, erratic; tough, cruel, bold, innovative, aloof, emotionally cool.

The Constellation Pisces or Pisces the Fishes:
February 21st to March 20th.

Seasonal characteristics: The winter ends, warmer weather approaches and life returns. Birds reappear and the melting snow in northern latitudes instils a very deep emotional feeling of re-birth. The sound of nature is heard again as streams and rivers swell and overflow. Food supplies run low and fasting is required, making physical energy low.

Personal characteristics: Sensitive, emotional, pliable, humble, kind, receptive, vague, sympathetic, compassionate, adaptable, receptive, intuitive, impressionable, superstitious, lacking willpower, indecisive, easily confused, careless, faithful, sacrificial, frail, warm hearted.

The Ancient Spirit

Interwoven within the astrological Earth-sky fabric was the belief that everything in nature was alive and every object controlled by its own independent spirit. Spirits were seen in rivers, lakes, woods, mountains, trees, animals, flowers, grass and birds. All objects possessed an essence, a purpose and everything became an object of worship or at the very least, objects of respect, including objects in the sky.

The Milky Way became a path for the soul leading to the spirit land. The Northern Lights were the dances of dead relatives in the realms above. The sky seen as a sacred entity was all but a universal belief and often related to the highest divinity. The sky god was a god of atmospheric phenomena, storms, rain, thunder and lightning, whose power for the good or ill of the people was extolled. In spite of his power, the sky god was only one of many deities. All the deities and symbols played a balancing act between humankind and nature. Our ancestors were close to nature in a way that is hard to imagine today.

The spirit of Mother Earth was particularly important and attracted the respect of peoples across the globe from North America through Siberia to Australia. The Celts attributed special powers to trees, which brought good fortune and protection. The Oak Tree and the Holly Tree were deified in Celtic mythology becoming the twin seasonal gods. These beliefs were signs of unconditional trust in the powers of nature and of a conviction that the powers of nature were so strong, they controlled human destiny.

Many cultures believed every mountain, lake or river had its own spirit owner, which owned the area and was in command of the animals and birds living there. The spirit owner could protect people who lived in that area as well as those who passed through it. Spirit owners were able to understand human speech and the myths associated with them say they had children, and one could obtain their goodwill with prayers and offerings.

Among peoples with hunting and fishing traditions, the daily interactions with their natural environment formed a unique worldview. Not only human beings but also all the animate and inanimate things of the world had souls. Theirs was an animist belief system, in which the environment was of primary importance. This ecologically minded, mythological view of the world and the cosmos provided a fascinating background for the development of myth and symbolism. If a hunting tradition were followed it would be sensible to maintain a close relationship with the spirits of hunted animals. If an agrarian tradition were followed it would be sensible to maintain a close relationship with the spirits of the land. The anthropomorphism of the signs of the zodiac fitted well in the prevailing culture of animism and images of the world were easily mirrored onto the heavens.

The Age of Aquarius

We live in the Age of Pisces and will enter the Age of Aquarius when the corresponding constellation sign slips a little farther back allowing the Sun to enter the zodiac sign of Aquarius at the spring equinox. This will occur in about 600 years' time. The Age of Pisces started around 68 BC and lasts until about 2597 AD when the Age of Aquarius begins. The much-heralded Age of Aquarius has not quite dawned. It received a premature welcome. We are living in the Age of Pisces, which replaced the Age of Aries over 2000 years ago.

The Age of Taurus began:	4539BC
The Age of Aries began:	1865BC
The Age of Pisces began:	0068BC
The Age of Aquarius begins:	2597AD
The Age of Capricorn begins:	4312AD
The Age of Sagittarius begins:	6271AD
The Age of Ophiuchus begins:	8598AD
The Age of Scorpio begins:	9876AD

Hipparchus re-discovered the precession of the equinoxes (already known in Babylonia and the Far East centuries earlier) at a time when astrological belief pervaded Mediterranean intellectual and religious life. The stars and planets were held to be living gods and their movements controlled all aspects of life. People believed in 'astral immortality', the idea that after death the human soul ascends up through the heavenly spheres to an afterlife in the pure and eternal world of the stars. Hipparchus's discovery of the precession made it clear that before the Greco-

Roman period, in which the spring equinox occurred in the constellation of Aries the Ram, the spring equinox had last been in Taurus the Bull. This discovery was an obvious signal: the precession of the equinox meant the death of the bull symbolising the end of the Age of Taurus.

The precession was believed to be caused by the new god and the new god naturally become the agent of death of the bull, hence the 'bull-slayer'. This is the origin of Mithras the cosmic bull-slayer (Roman religion). His killing of the bull symbolised his supreme power, the power to move the entire universe which he had demonstrated by shifting the cosmic sphere in such a way the spring equinox had moved out of Taurus the Bull.

The bull slayer lives on today in the Spanish bullring. The killing of the bull stems from the Mithric movement of the cosmic sphere. The original belief underlying the Spanish corrida de toros has been lost even among the Spanish. Many scholars attribute it to the Roman Circus where men battled with wild beasts and among them, wild bulls. While the modern corrida de toros has obvious Moorish connections its origins stem from the Greco-Roman period.

If for just one moment you could replace the 'living bull' with the 'symbolic bull' of the cosmic sphere, the meaning of this tradition becomes clear. The matador with a muleta in his left hand and a sword in his right hand throws himself upon the bull and strikes the bull in the nape of the neck: descabellar. It is Aries replacing Taurus. Look how the matador is dressed, observe his behaviour and attitude and look how the bull is weakened and overcome. The bull ruled the ring (the cosmos) and now the matador struts triumphantly like a ram after the exchange is completed.

The number of bulls in each corrida is eight which also fits the quarter and cross quarter day symmetry. Given the influence in the Greco-Roman period of astrology, a god possessing such a literally world shaking power would clearly have been eminently worthy of such practices since he had control over the cosmos and would automatically have power over the astrological forces determining life on Earth.

Palmistry

The signs of the zodiac held sway over every aspect of life and their power cannot be overestimated. The ancient art of palmistry is ruled by movements within the signs of the zodiac.

Palmistry is based on the analysis of lines, pads, textures, shape and colour of the hand. Originating in India and China over 2000 years ago it was skilfully practised by the ancient Greeks. Introduced into Europe as a magical art with astrological links it was quickly taken up and later included in the curriculum of some universities (as was astrology). Each finger on the hand is ruled by a particular planet: index finger: Jupiter, middle finger: Saturn, third finger: Sun, and little finger: Mercury. The fleshy pads at the base of the fingers are known as the mounts and again named after the planets.

Tarot

Tarot is also steeped in Earth sky symbolism. The Major Arcane contains twenty-two cards full of imagery and symbolism. The Magician has his right hand holding a wand pointing towards heaven and his left hand pointing to the Earth. The High Priestess is Isis the Moon Goddess, with the waxing crescent Moon at her feet, the solar cross on her breast and the horned Moon her crown. The Empress is Venus, and the Emperor, Jupiter. The Hierphant is the masculine spiritual ruler on Earth. The Lovers are Adam and Eve backed by the Tree of Knowledge and the Tree of Life. The Star is a naked woman on a shoreline and the star above her is surrounded by seven lesser stars: Sirius surrounded by Pleiades; and the woman is Aquarius.

All are linked to the Earth and Sky. All are ancient signs directing our attention to layers of unconscious energy hidden deep within our mind. The cosmos supported all social, philosophical and religious structures and I do not believe in the 21st century we are about to lose the spiritual significance of this cosmic heritage.

Astrology

I am often informed astrology is 'rubbish'. Sceptics object to the work of even serious astrologers without first examining either the history or the evidence. They simply throw out the challenge: 'prove it'. The influence of the Moon is considerable. It controls the tides and over half of all living creatures on Earth, especially tidal invertebrates which set their biological clock to the rhythm of the Moon. Lunatics are so called because the power of the Full Moon sends them a bit crazy. An increase in death from heart failure occurs during a sunspot maxima period because solar activity increases the strength of the geomagnetic field, which affects the heart. These two celestial bodies have a great effect on life and behaviour.

A standard dictionary definition of astrology would say 'a pseudoscience professing to foretell the future and interpret the influence of heavenly bodies upon the destinies of men.' Such dictionary definitions are far from adequate in describing the complexities of astrology. The narrow view of portraying astrology as a fortune-telling craft would not even have applied several thousand years ago. Astrology is a serious study and attempts to understand human behaviour more than the foretelling of events. Astrology's predictive power lies in offering suitable choices and possible outcomes based on personal and cosmic energies. The purely predictive Sun-sign horoscope columns printed in newspapers are, as their authors would confess, a bit of fun.

The word 'astrology' is derived from 'Astrologia' in Latin and ancient Greek. It is a composite of the word 'Astro' meaning 'Star' and the word 'Logos' meaning 'discourse'. Astrology has been practised in many ways over the centuries. In the beginning the Sun, and more importantly the Moon were believed to be the only major influences on human affairs. Eventually, more celestial items were added, such as planets, zodiac signs, bright stars, asteroids and countless astronomical factors. All are linked directly to the heavens and fall under the grand term 'cosmic influences'. Astrology was originally an attempt to formulate order in the universe and to draw from it a sense of relative security.

Today, astrology is the science of the effects of the planets' movements on our lives and all things. Astrology is based on astronomy in that astrologers need to know the correct positions of the planets at any given time, as well as the 'positions' of the zodiacal fixed star signs in relation to any location on Earth at any given time. Once the correct positions of the signs and planets are known, the astrologer constructs a chart representing these positions called a 'birth chart' or 'natal chart'. By reading this chart you can discover much about yourself. Astrology in its wider sense offers another level or another layer of consciousness by which we may gain psychological and spiritual insights. Astrology may be viewed as a quest for deep, meaningful perceptions about life and ourselves in general. Astrology may be used to understand ourselves and our karma for this life.

History

Markings on Ice Age bones suggest humans were aware of lunar cycles over 35 000 years ago. During the upper Paleolithic period our ancestors observed and reported the cycles of the Moon by nicks cut in reindeer bones and in mammoth ivory. The part of the world located between the Tigris and Euphrates rivers provided the first astrological observatories. The Sumerians, who settled there around 6000 years ago constructed a most unusual feature, the ziggurat, a pyramidal stepped tower and the progenitor of the great pyramids. Its flat summit was used by the priests to study the night skies.

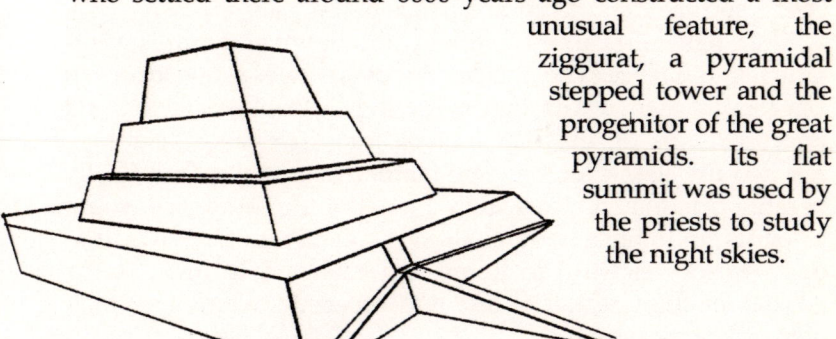

Fig 15
MESOPOTAMIAN ZIGGURAT The ziggurat was a cosmic axis, a vertical bond between heaven, Earth and the underworld, and a horizontal bond between the land. It was built on seven levels, representing the seven 'heavens', the seven planets, the seven metals and their corresponding colours.

The Sumerians left behind an extensive library of cuneiform tablets providing detailed records of their astrological knowledge. The Chaldeans became the great ancient astrologers because their measurements of celestial motion were the most accurate. Stonehenge, Callanish, Carac and other European megalithic observatories may have been as accurate, but nothing was left in writing.

The tablets of Sargon of Akkad dating from 2350 BC confirm the astrologer priests had identified omens in solar eclipses. However, they recorded more information about lunar eclipses and must have regarded these events with great respect as their calculations were accurate to within minutes of a degree. The Akkadians conquered Sumeria and incorporated translations of the Sumerian astrological records into their own writings. They worshipped the Sun, Moon and Venus, but used all the planets up to Saturn. By 2000 BC Sumeria was replaced by Babylonia. The Babylonian astrologers raised astrology to yet further heights with the 'invention' of the zodiac and further accurate astronomical calculations. The theory of the ecliptic divided into twelve thirty-degree sections or zodiac signs was completed by 540 BC. Early astrology was not directly personal. It was 'judicial' and dealt with grand-scale events such as wars, floods and affairs of the state.

The Chaldeans carried astrology into Egypt and more importantly into Greece. The ancient Egyptians never developed an advanced system of astrology involving vast tables of factors and interpretations as the Babylonians did. In Greece, astrology reached the classic look we are familiar with today and finally became personal. It also acquired most of the details we would recognise in today's traditional horoscope. From Greece, astrology spread westward to Rome and eastward to India under Alexander the Great. The east and especially China had their own astrological systems.

Astrology declined in Europe due to suppression by the Church but reappeared again during the Renaissance when scholars began to investigate old manuscripts and ancient knowledge, especially that of the Greeks. Astrological themes appeared in stained glass windows of cathedrals, in facades of public buildings and art. Leonardo da Vinci drew illustrations associating astrological symbols with parts of the body. Martin Luther supported astrology and wrote a preface to the work of astrologer Johannes Lichtenberger.

Shakespeare was obviously a little sceptical of astrology's power to influence human actions: 'The fault, dear Brutus, is not in our stars, But in ourselves, that we are underlings.' (Julius Caesar.) Shakespeare also helped to popularise astrology by inserting astrological references in almost all of his plays. Johannes Kepler established the fact that planets move in elliptical orbits around Sun and discovered the three famous laws of planetary motion which bear his name. Kepler was also a gifted astrologer and mystic as was Sir Isaac Newton. Kepler linked planetary orbit spheres with geometric solids and wrote 'Music of the Spheres'. Since then astrology has had its ups and downs but has continued to evolve until the present day.

Astrological Birth Chart

There are many applications of astrology. Natal astrology links solar, lunar and planetary positions at the moment of birth with the personality of the individual. Synastry looks at compatibility. Astro-meteorology deals with earthquakes, volcanic eruptions and climate conditions. Horary astrology interposes specific questions in terms of the chart erected, to be answered with relevance to that moment in time. Today we have Medical astrology, Financial astrology, Healing astrology, and so the list goes on.

An individual birth chart is drawn in the form of two concentric circles. The zodiac signs occupy the outside circle and proceed clockwise. The house divisions occupy the inner circle and proceed anti clockwise. The position of the planets relative to the time and place of birth are mapped accordingly on the diagram. Each planet fits not only a zodiac sign but also a 'house', of which there are twelve on the Earth framework. The interaction of the planets, signs and houses creates a complete picture of the personality, as individual as a fingerprint. The final image presented is only part of the interpretive process as the astrologer's own skill and intuition play a major role.

The subdivisions made to aid interpretation are divided into four Elements: Earth, Air, Fire and Water; three Qualities: Cardinal, Fixed and Mutable; and two magnetic states: Positive and Negative. Influences below the horizon are unconscious aspects of the personality and those above the horizon are conscious aspects of the personality. The birth chart is not a magic mirror which reflects every detail of your character and life. The chart is not a map of one's fate or unalterable future, but a map with many roads and forks from which to choose. It is up to you to live up to the potential of the chart. The chart by itself, regardless of how good or bad the factors are does not mean those things have to reflect your life. Some factors will reflect while others will not. There may be many things not presented in your chart, factors usually attributed to external influences. Some factors may not seem relevant to you at all, often because they are not brought out during the early years or simply because they are blocked by external influences.

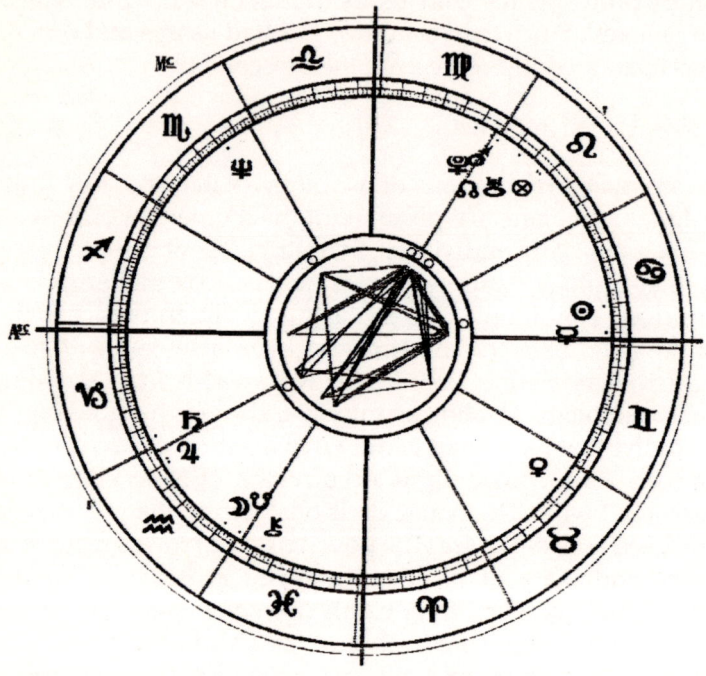

Fig 16 TRADITIONAL ZODIAC BIRTH CHART
This is the Birth Chart of Diana Francis Spencer born at 7.45 pm on July 1st 1961 at Park House near Sandringham, Norfolk.

The non-astrological influences that can block or inhibit your potential expressions and talents indicated in a birth chart are: social and political systems, environments, traditions, family circumstances, religions, institutions and spouses. For centuries society was mostly patriarchal and women could not reflect the potential talents in their charts. Women were forced to be submissive and behave with unreasonable respect and deference to men. They were confined to areas such as cooking, household duties and rearing children and were not allowed to attend universities, to become doctors, lawyers, merchants, artists, composers or many of the other professions. Today, women are 'allowed' to work in almost all the areas once dominated by men. Clearly, in the many millions of women's charts in the past there were certainly the same numbers of potential talents for becoming doctors, lawyers, engineers, and politicians as today. It would be absurd to think so many charts would have only factors indicating a talent for just housework.

There are numerous other examples of the same problem of external influences hindering potential chart expressions, which affect men as well. In coastline areas, the main profession is fishing. The men go out to sea and fish and preoccupy themselves with all the activities related to fishing, boat and net maintenance and repair. It is unlikely for a son to say to his father he suddenly wants to break the family tradition and become a ballet dancer, even if his chart indicates all the potential for a great ballet dancer. Generation after generation the same profession was passed on from father to son that forced all other members of the family to conform to the fishing business. Hereditary traits are yet another external factor. There is enough evidence suggesting the birth chart cannot explain every trait, event and circumstance in your life.

Traditional Zodiac Astrology Details

Sign	Type	Date	Element	Magnetism	Quality	Ruler
Aries	Ram	Mar-21	Fire	Pos	Cardinal	Mars
Taurus	Bull	April-20	Earth	Neg	Fixed	Venus
Gemini	Twins	May-21	Air	Pos	Mutable	Mercury
Cancer	Crab	June-21	Water	Neg	Cardinal	Moon
Leo	Lion	July-23	Fire	Pos	Fixed	Sun
Virgo	Virgin	Aug-23	Earth	Neg	Mutable	Mercury
Libra	Scales	Sept-23	Air	Pos	Cardinal	Venus
Scorpio	Scorpion	Oct-23	Water	Neg	Fixed	Mars-Pluto
Sagittarius	Centaur	Nov-22	Fire	Pos	Mutable	Jupiter
Capricorn	Goat	Dec-22	Earth	Neg	Cardinal	Saturn
Aquarius	Water-carrier	Jan-20	Air	Pos	Fixed	Uranus-Saturn
Pisces	Fish	Feb-19	Water	Neg	Mutable	Neptune-Jupiter

Different Systems

There are many different astrological systems. Traditional western astrology, described above is the one you are probably most familiar with. Other systems include Indian, Nirayana or Vedic astrology, Chinese or Meng astrology, western new zodiac or constellational astrology and Celtic astrology.

Traditional western astrology uses the twelve sign tropical zodiac. Indian, Nirayana or Vedic astrology uses the twelve sign sidereal movable zodiac; new zodiac astrology uses the constellational, sidereal movable zodiac. Chinese or Meng astrology is a lunar-based system completely different from the others using Moon signs and the sixty-year lunar cycle. Celtic astrology also has a lunar-based zodiac.

Indian, Nirayana, Vedic Astrology

Vedic astrology differs from Western or Tropical astrology mainly in that most western astrology uses the fixed zodiac as opposed to the moving zodiac. Because of the gradual tilting of the Earth on its axis, the zodiac appears to be moving at the rate of one degree approximately every seventy-two years. Currently, the relative or movable zodiac is out of alignment with the fixed zodiac by roughly twenty-three degrees, which is almost one whole sign of the zodiac. Vedic astrology sticks with that original star based zodiac and thus another term to describe Vedic astrology is 'sidereal astrology'.

The signs the planets are in are one important part of astrology. Because the two systems are skewed from each other by nearly one whole sign, most people's Sun sign, which you can get from the newspaper each day is usually one sign out when the chart is refigured using Vedic astrology. The first surprise using Vedic is that you are no longer the Sun sign you always thought you were. This happens with many charts, since the signs have actually moved by twenty-three degrees in the last 2000 years, relative to the Vernal Equinox.

Vedic astrology has a great number of techniques for studying the charts once they are cast. The 'dashas' or 'planetary ruling periods' system which is a part of the Vedic system gives Vedic astrologers a tool for predicting the trends, changes and events in your life regarding the order in which they will take place. Vedic astrologers are less limited to talking about your general overall self (personality and counselling) and can get more deeply into what is going to happen in your life. Signs are called 'Rashis' (raw-shees) in Sanskrit.

Vedic Zodiac Astrology Details

The table shows the signs with their rulers, Sanskrit names and symbols.

Sign	Sanskrit	Date	Meaning	Type	Sex	Mobility	Lord
Aries	Mesha	Apr-12	Ram	Fire	M	Movable	Mars
Taurus	Vrishaba	May-12	Bull	Earth	F	Fixed	Venus
Gemini	Mithuna	Jun-12	Couple embracing	Air	M	Common	Mercury
Cancer	Karkata	Jul-12	Crab/Circle	Water	F	Movable	Moon
Leo	Simha	Aug-12	Lion	Fire	M	Fixed	Sun
Virgo	Kanya	Sep-1	Virgin/Daughter	Earth	F	Common	Mercury
Libra	Thula	Oct-12	Balance/Weight	Air	M	Movable	Venus
Scorpio	Vrishchika	Nov-11	Scorpion	Water	F	Fixed	Mars
Sagittarius	Dhanus	Dec-12	Bow (weapon)	Fire	M	Common	Jupiter
Capricorn	Makara	Jan-11	Shark/Alligator	Earth	F	Movable	Saturn
Aquarius	Kumbha	Feb-1	Pot/Jug	Air	M	Fixed	Saturn
Pisces	Meena	Mar-12	Fishes	Water	F	Common	Jupiter

The signs are the same as those used in western astrology. However, the understanding of what the signs do, the demigods behind them, who controsl them, vary and are greatly augmented in Vedic astrology.

New Zodiac Astrology

Like Vedic astrology, new zodiac astrology uses the moving or sidereal zodiac. It differs from Vedic astrology in that new zodiac astrology uses the actual star constellation of the true zodiac. In the real zodiac the Sun does not spend equal time in each zodiac sign therefore the sign divisions are unequal. For example, the Sun spends forty-five days in Virgo while only six days in Scorpio. Again, the first surprise when using new zodiac astrology is that you are no longer the Sun sign you always thought you were, indeed you may even be a completely new zodiac sign: Ophiuchus. Three other constellations also encroach upon the zodiac: Orion, Sextans and Cetus. A portion of the Sun actually enters Cetus around March 27th.

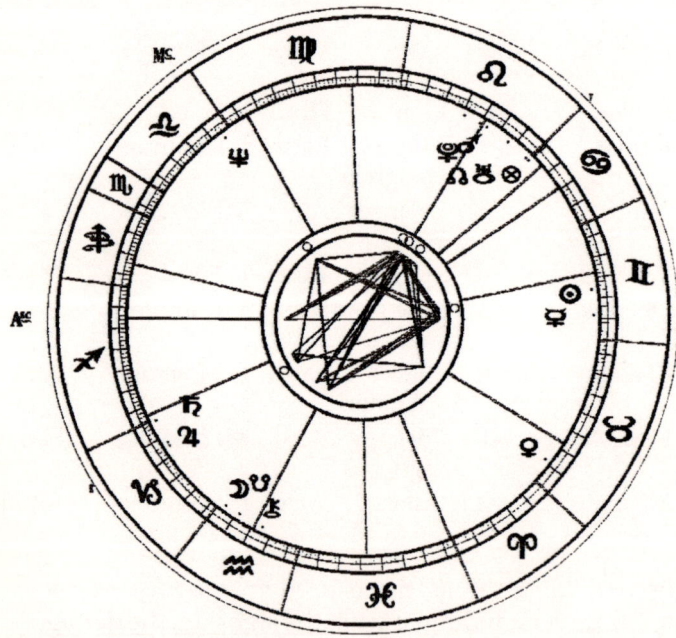

Fig 17 NEW ZODIAC BIRTH CHART
Compare this New Zodiac Birth Cart of Princess Diana with the traditional Birth Chart on page 105.

New Zodiac Astrology Details

Sign	Type	Date	Element	Mag	Quality	Ruler
Pisces	Fish	Mar-12	Water	Neg	Mutable	Neptune-Jupiter
Cetus		Mar-27				
Aries	Ram	Apr-18	Fire	Pos	Cardinal	Mars
Taurus	Bull	May-14	Earth	Neg	Fixed	Venus
Orion		June-18 to-20				
Gemini	Twins	June-21	Air	Pos	Mutable	Mercury
Cancer	Crab	July-21	Water	Neg	Cardinal	Moon
Leo	Lion	Aug-10	Fire	Pos	Fixed	Sun
Sextans		Sep-3				
Virgo	Virgin	Sep-16	Earth	Neg	Mutable	Mercury
Libra	Scales	Oct-31	Air	Pos	Cardinal	Venus
Scorpio	Scorpion	Nov-23	Water	Neg	Fixed	Mars-Pluto
Ophiuchus	Serpent	Nov-29	Water	Neg	Mutable	Pluto-Jupiter
Sagittarius	Centaur	Dec-17	Fire	Pos	Mutable	Jupiter
Capricorn	Goat	Jan-19	Earth	Neg	Cardinal	Saturn
Aquarius	Carrier	Feb-16	Air	Pos	Fixed	Uranus-Saturn

The Sun approaches Orion to about 2 degrees during this period.

The Sun approaches Sextans to about 2 degrees on this day.

The Sun approaches Cetus to less than 0.5 degrees on this day: part of the Sun but not all of it enters Cetus.

Chinese or Meng Astrology

Chinese astrology is based on the sixty-year lunar cycle so there are no Sun signs only Moon signs! Chinese astrology is quite different from the astrological systems you may be familiar with. The Chinese zodiac divides people into twelve personality types: the twelve animals. There are also five elements: metal, wood, water, fire and earth, which determine the characteristics and the 'fate' of people. These five elements are represented by the five planets Venus, Jupiter, Mercury, Mars and Saturn with the same names in Chinese. Individually each element's sign appears only once every sixty years calculated by multiplying twelve signs by five elements in line with the lunar cycle.

Fig 18 YIN AND YANG

> When some things are deemed beautiful other things become ugly.
> When things are deemed good other things become bad.
> Existence and non-existence create each other.
> Difficult and easy produce each other.
> Long and short are fashioned from each other.
> High and low contrast each other.
> Before and behind follow each other.

In the glyph for Yin and Yang you will see there is a little bit of Yin in the Yang area and little bit of Yang in the Yin area. Even when the Goddess is being the Sun there is a little part of her that is being the Moon. Meng's five element cosmos is like the game 'Rock, Paper Scissors', each element being good for one element and bad for another. Water nourishes Wood, but it puts out Fire. Every element has at least one other element that strengthens it and at least one element that destroys it. Water is held or strengthened by Metal but Earth absorbs or weakens Water.

The Nourishment Cycle: Earth carries Metal; Metal holds Water; Water nourishes Wood; Wood feeds Fire; Fire creates Earth (ashes).

The Destruction Cycle: Earth absorbs Water; Water drowns Fire; Fire melts Metal; Metal cuts Wood; Wood parts Earth.

Combine the Elements with the Qualities of Yin and Yang and you will find the Ten Heavenly Stems: expressed as colours, the Stems help to modify and define the characteristics of the Meng:

When Fire is Yin it is Purple, When Fire is Yang it is Red
When Earth is Yin it is Gold, When Earth is Yang it is Yellow
When Metal is Yin it is Silver, When Metal is Yang it is White
When Water is Yin it is Grey, When Water is Yang it is Black
When Wood is Yin it is Blue, When Wood is Yang it is Green

Although it may not seem immediately apparent, the polarity of the elements is a crucial point in Chinese Astrology. The 'Animals' are more properly referred to as The Twelve Branches: Rat, Ox, Tiger, Rabbit, Dragon, Snake, Horse, Goat, Monkey, Rooster, Dog, and Pig.

Animal Years

Years named for the animals of the Chinese zodiac. Which animal are you?

Rat	1912	1924	1936	1948	1960	1972	1984	1996	2008	2020
Ox	1913	1925	1937	1949	1961	1973	198	1997	2009	2021
Tiger	1914	1926	1938	1950	1962	1974	1986	1998	2010	2022
Rabbit	1915	1927	1939	1951	1963	1975	1987	1999	2011	2023
Dragon	1916	1928	1940	1952	1964	1976	1988	2000	2012	2024
Snake	1917	1929	1941	1953	1965	1977	1989	2001	2013	2025
Horse	1918	1930	1942	1954	1966	1978	1990	2002	2014	2026
Goat	1919	1931	1943	1955	1967	1979	1991	2003	2003	2015
Monkey	1920	1932	1944	1956	1968	1980	1992	2004	2004	2016
Rooster	1921	1933	1945	1957	1969	1981	1993	2005	2005	2017
Dog	1922	1934	1946	1958	1970	1982	1994	2006	2005	2018
Pig	1923	1935	1947	1959	1971	1983	1995	2007	2007	2019

According to the Chinese calendar, the year has 354 days and twelve lunar months, about half of them with thirty days and the other half with twenty-nine days. In order to make the months correspond with the movements of the Earth around the Sun, a thirteenth month is inserted every two or three years. The New Year begins on the New Moon and may occur at any time from January 1st to February 19th, inclusive. If you were born between these dates you will have to consult a detailed listing to find your Chinese animal year sign.

Chinese Lunar Sign Details

Sign	Time	Month	Element	Quality
Rat	11-pm	November-22	Water	Yang
Ox	1-am	December-22	Water	Yin
Tiger	3-am	January-21	Wood	Yang
Rabbit	5-am	February-20	Wood	Yin
Dragon	7-am	March-20	Wood	Yang
Snake	9-am	April-20	Fire	Yin
Horse	11-am	May-21	Fire	Yang
Goat	1-pm	June-22	Fire	Yin
Monkey	3-pm	July-22	Metal	Yang
Rooster	5-pm	August-22	Metal	Yin
Dog	7-pm	September-23	Metal	Yang
Pig	9-pm	October-23	Water	Yin

The element, Earth is not used in the fixed elements because the Earth is symbolically composed of the other four elements. When you combine the Five Elements with the Twelve Branches you get appellation: 'Yellow Dragon' and 'Black Serpent'. When the Element combines with the Branch's energy the branch's Yin or Yang quality causes the Stem to become apparent. 'Earth Dragon' would always be expressed as 'Yellow Dragon' because the Dragon is a Yang Branch. 'Earth Rabbit' would always be expressed as 'Gold Rabbit or Hare' because the Rabbit is a Yin Branch. A total of sixty combinations are possible between the Branches and the Stems. Every Branch is paired with a Stem in the cycle for the Meng. The Cycle begins with Black Rat. Because there are Ten Stems and Twelve Branches, the Stems will begin repeating at the eleventh Branch, Dog.

These are the building blocks of Chinese astrology. It is quite a different system. Every two-hour period is ruled by a different Branch Stem combination known as the first Pillar. Every day is ruled by a different Branch Stem combination known as the second Pillar. Every season, or month is defined by a Branch Stem combination known as the Third Pillar. Finally, every year is ruled by a Branch Stem combination known as the Fourth Pillar. There are four established Pillars that can be used to describe the state of the Universe at the time of your birth. These eight characters comprise your Chinese 'Birth Chart' also called the Bazi. As in western astrology, your Bazi can be used not only to describe your character and personality but also to determine compatibility and identify favourable times for certain activities and pursuits, to determine the flows of your own life.

Knowledge of the Five Elements is a preparation for proficiency in Feng Shui, the art of geomantic placement, which helps the Ch'i flow more gracefully in your life, bringing satisfaction and prosperity. (In the West, Feng Shui is erroneously used out of context as simply an interior design tool!) The 'I Ching' or book of changes whose sixty-four hexagrams are based on the combination of the eight trigrams are based on the same five Elements.

Celtic Astrology

The Celts left no written records describing their mathematics or techniques, aside from Oghams and glyphs. They were an 'oral tradition' society rather than a written one. Therefore, understandably a little confusion exists regarding interpretation. The Celtic zodiac is based on the cycle of the Moon with the year divided into thirteen lunar months and each associated with a tree sacred to the Druids. The Druids believed the human race originally descended from the trees. Each tree had particular magical qualities. They encoded these mysteries in a secret shamanic alphabet, known as the Ogham, the origin of which is ascribed to Ogma, the Celtic God of Poetry.

The thirteen tree months each correspond to a tree, a letter of the Ogham alphabet, a Guardian Animal and a Celtic god. The Celts and Druids used a thirteen-month lunar-based calendar similar in many ways to that used by the Chinese.

Celtic Thirteen Lunar Sign Details

Ogham	Tree-Sign	Date	Animal-Guardian	God
Beithe	Birch	Dec-7	White-Stag	Lugh
Luis	Rowan	Jan-4	Green-Dragon	Brigid
Nion	Ash	Feb-1	Sea-Horse	Magician
Fern	Alder	Mar-1	The-Fox	Bran
Sail	Willow	Mar-29	The-Hare	Moon
Uath	Hawthorn	Apr-26	The-Owl	Olwen
Duir	Oak	May-24	The-Wren	Dagda
Tinne	Holly	Jun-22	The-Unicorn	Gavannon

Coll	Hazel	Jul-20	Rainbow-Salmon	Manannan
Muin	Vine	Aug-17	White-Swan	Danaan
Gort	Ivy	Sep-14	The-Butterfly	Guinevere
Ngetal	Reed	Oct-12	The-Dog	Pwyll
Ruis	Elder	Nov-8	The-Raven	Cailleach

Interested?

If you decide to consult an astrologer to have your birth chart interpreted, which astrological system do you choose? In a stressful and uncertain world, any system of self-development that may bring personal and spiritual insights is useful. Try the astrological system you feel most intuitively comfortable with. If you want to compare and contrast, try other systems. All will reveal some truth. Most importantly, do not build your life around your birth chart. Astrology is one tool, one method among hundreds which can bring a deeper understanding of yourself and help your energy flow smoothly. Everything in your life, as in nature, must be kept in balance so that natural harmony is maintained and karma is achieved.

Confirmation

Human knowledge advances. New theories supersede existing theories. These theories are eventually superseded by newer theories. Each generation becomes attached to the existing knowledge paradigm. Society buys into prevailing theories so much so, the theories become a part of society's own internal psychology. Mainstream scientists buy into prevailing scientific theories and many become blind, religiously scientific fundamentalists. Many astrologers too adopt the same attitude. Rather than embrace new ideas, they condemn new ideas outright without serious investigation.

The success or failure of a theory becomes associated with the success or failure of one's career and many people have their lives invested in their career. People struggled to learn complicated things and as students, their lives have depended upon whether they could pass an examination and regurgitate 'meaningless' facts. People take their hard won knowledge seriously and if someone questions its validity their psychological security becomes threatened and they become defensive.

Astrology is at a crossroads and must evolve in the light of new understanding. Astrology should use the 'best' of ancient wisdom and combine this, if applicable, with the insights of modern wisdom. By doing so, serious astrology has a bright future and will be accessed more and more by society. Serious astrology can be, and is a valuable and useful tool in many areas of life. Popular astrology will continue in the same 'luck, love, health, wealth' format. I do not have a problem with this. Individuals need relief, a little bit of fun and so long as popular astrology is recognised for what it is, I have no problem with it.

Traditional twelve-zodiac astrology and its associated personality characteristics were closely related to seasonal changes. I know the movement of the planets affect conditions within the solar magnetic field and this disturbs the geomagnetic field affecting life on Earth, including human behaviour and personality. Recent evidence extends the boundaries of the solar magnetic field to include the stars themselves. Bodies tens of thousands of light years distant affect the cycles of the planets, which in turn affect the solar magnetic field and thus the geomagnetic field. The patterns, rhythms, circles and cycles of the cosmos affect everyone.

Bio-resonant systems are able to tune into the rhythm and harmony of the cosmos. If we are to provide an accurate description of the energy interchange between the macrocosm and the microcosm, the actual star constellations as they appear from Earth should be taken into account. I am aware the influence from distant stars is small but as chaos theory shows, a small change in initial conditions can produce chaotic and fundamentally unpredictable changes in later conditions. The following example is often quoted: a butterfly flaps its wings in Tokyo and three days later a hurricane develops in Chicago.

Bio-Resonance

The nervous system is stimulated by electrochemical activity. Therefore an external electromagnetic force can influence the nervous system and other biological structures. This is the principle of Magnetic Resonance Imaging (MRI) and the source of the danger associated with overhead power cables. (MRI) is an imaging technique used primarily in medical settings to produce images of the inside of the human body. MRI is based on the principles of nuclear magnetic resonance (NMR). The technique is called magnetic resonance imaging rather than nuclear magnetic resonance imaging (NMRI) because of the negative connotations associated with the word 'nuclear'. The human body is primarily fat and water. Fat and water have many hydrogen atoms that make the human body approximately sixty-three per cent hydrogen atoms. Hydrogen nuclei have an NMR signal. For these reasons MRI primarily images the NMR signal from the hydrogen nuclei, because within each cell there are molecules of water. Each water molecule has one oxygen and two hydrogen atoms. If we pass through the electron cloud the hydrogen nucleus comprises a single proton. The proton possesses a property called spin, which can be thought of as a small magnetic field, and it is this that causes the nucleus to produce an NMR signal.

Magnetic fields associated with overhead power cables are difficult to shield and easily penetrate buildings and people. The biological effects of power frequency fields due to the magnetic component of the field have been the subject of much controversy. Power frequency fields cause biological effects via the electromagnetic fields they induce in the body. The fields or currents induced in the body are low but if one is continually exposed to them, leukaemia or other carcinogenic disorders can occur.

Bio-resonant sub-systems within a biological structure can detect small changes in the Earth's magnetic field. The geomagnetic field fluctuates constantly and cyclically by interacting with the Sun's magnetic field. The Moon and planets also interact and create fluctuations within the solar magnetic field. The interaction is very complicated. At a basic level, we know biological systems utilise the Sun's magnetic field. Birds use it as a compass to navigate. Bees use a similar electromagnetic method for navigation too. Many birds navigate at night using the position of the stars.

Experiments carried out at Manchester University revealed students who had been blindfolded and transported dozens of miles could point north and give the direction of the university. These few examples support evidence of a bio-resonant biological component. Ultimately there are few hiding places from the effects of the geomagnetic field. Our nervous system is constantly subjected to these changes and research (Percy Seymour) suggests magnetic variation within the geomagnetic field may become etched on our nervous system while still in the womb. This may be responsible for the traditional astrological seasonal personality traits.

Signal Reception

Bio-resonance systems are able to tune into particular astro-resonant cycles or signals. We are consciously unaware of the fluctuating and cyclical nature of the geomagnetic field. Furthermore, we are actually unlikely to be affected by it unless we are tuned into a certain frequency or cycle. The concept is similar to that of your radio or television receiver. By turning the dial, or pushing buttons on the remote control unit you can tune into the station of your choice. Prior to the 19th century, electromagnetic waves or fields were unknown and we now known the universe to be replete with fields. There is no such thing as nothing. There is no empty space.

Electromagnetic fields (among other things) are everywhere, interconnected and bathing the cosmos. The Moon and planets subtly alter the magnetic flux patterns within the solar system by interacting with the Sun's magnetic field. Astrologers recognise this energy, which can be positive (harmonious) or negative (inharmonious). One example already quoted is that of the geomagnetic field being affected by solar mass ejecta during sunspot maxima. This affects the human heart (research from

Israel) and would be considered an inharmonious energy. The Moon moves thousands of millions of tons of water in and out of Morecambe Bay twice a day. The human body is primarily fat and water and the Moon's pull affects us all in subtle ways. The Moon also causes tides in the upper atmosphere, which give rise to electric currents that generate the lunar daily magnetic variation. The position and movement of the heavenly bodies as seen from Earth at the time of birth are linked to personality characteristics and behaviour.

Much statistical research has been undertaken in this field, primarily by Michel Gauquelin and the cosmos / human connection has also been investigated by Hans Eysenck and Jeff Mayo. Their results are too copious to be dealt with here but they do provide a body of evidence in support of serious astrological theory and practice.

Star Connection

One piece of apparatus left behind on the Moon by Apollo 11, 14 and 15 missions was a retro-reflector. A retro-reflector is a tough, highly polished mirror used for reflecting light. A laser beam sited on Earth is directed at the retro-reflector on the surface of the Moon and reflected back to Earth. Using this technique, we can calculate the distance of the Moon from the Earth very accurately to within one hundredth of an inch. In 1994 American and German scientists analysed the lunar laser ranging measurements and computed the Moon's exact orbital motion over a twenty-five year period. The distance of the Moon was recorded to within a fraction of an inch for every minute of every day over twenty-five years.

When the laser ranging data had been analysed and matched against the traditionally computed orbit of the Moon, minor orbital anomalies were discovered that were not expected. The orbital distortions were small but the Moon now and again appeared to wobble. Initially no explanation for this orbital distortion could be found. The lunar perturbations, distortions, wobbles, vibrations and oscillations recorded were small and one by one, the possible effects of the planets and other objects in the solar system were eliminated, i.e. they were not responsible for the Moon's deviations.

An influence outside of the solar system was affecting the Earth/Moon system and the distortion of the Moon's orbit was traced to the stars. Stars hundreds of thousands of light years distant affect the orbit of the Moon and Earth! These stars will certainly affect the orbits of the other planets in the solar system, especially the larger gas giants. It has been known for some years, distant stars displace cometary material from the Oort cloud, a no-mans land at the edge of the solar system, sending comets crashing into the inner solar system. The distant stars affect us all. Every little wobble or variation, no matter how large or small is indirectly picked up and noted by bio-resonant subsystems, in biological structures and just like magnetic tape is stored and retrieved when the same resonant signals occur in the future.

Conclusion

The Sun moves against the background of stars and constellations. It depends on the relative position of the Earth and the Sun where the Sun appears to be among the stars. The traditional twelve signs of the zodiac were fixed about 2000 years ago by the Babylonians. They divided the zodiac into twelve equal parts and named the parts according to the constellations they recognised at that time. The signs of the zodiac were linked to times of the year according to where the Sun was at those times.

Since then, several things have happened to confuse traditional astrological signs and astronomical constellations. The astronomical constellations and their boundaries were officially fixed by the International Astronomical Union in 1930 and they do not coincide exactly with the constellations that were recognised by the Babylonians. The division of the sky into eighty-eight constellations does not give special consideration to the zodiac. Also, the astronomical constellations through which the zodiac is placed do not all contain equal parts of the zodiac. The zodiac now traverses thirteen rather than twelve constellations and the Sun passes within five degrees of three additional constellations. Furthermore, the constellations are continually slipping due to the precession of the equinox.

Modern twelve-zodiac astrology effectively links the astrological signs to the seasons and not the stars. Originally, twelve-zodiac astrology linked the astrological signs to the seasons and the stars. Aries the Ram has moved by about thirty-five degrees or just over one astrological sign since the time of the Babylonians. During the Greco-Roman period (the origins of the tropical zodiac) the astrological zodiac alluded to the star constellations. Indeed, their astrological theory claimed the movement of the stars and planets controlled every aspect of intellectual and religious life. We know the stars, Moon, planets and other bodies within the solar system vibrate the solar magnetic field which affects the geomagnetic field and produces / activates bio-resonant signals in biological structures, including human beings. 21st century holistic insights are providing an underpinning knowledge to support astrology but it is complicated. My hope is those who are involved in serious astrology do not let their preconceptions lead to a polarisation of views. There is no need to feel threatened by new ideas. Let us value intellectual difference and diversity in a positive and non-threatening way.

Part Three

My Blue Heaven: Glimpsing The Invisible

How to Observe

Creature Comforts Checklist

- A sun lounger, portable sun bed or reclining chair
- Warm clothing. In winter, I wear full body Arctic thermals, Arctic boots and a Russian hat I bought in Moscow
- A flask containing your favourite hot drink
- Insect repellent in summer and a cool drink
- Mobile telephone for isolated areas
- Blanket, bone and a drink for Red (or your pet's needs)

You can observe the sky at any time. There is always something interesting to see: changing cloud formations, colourful twilights, the Sun rising and setting. Even above the city's bright lights the Moon, Venus, Jupiter and the brightest stars are visible. The sky offers you the greatest show on Earth, is free, available most of the time, can lift your spirits and make you forget all about your Earthly troubles.

Serious night sky observation requires a dark location away from artificial streetlights: perhaps your garden, local park or better, a trip to the country. Long and all night observation sessions need preparation, especially on cold, dark nights. The most important point to remember in winter is to wrap up warm when observing at night, especially if you intend to stay out until the early morning hours. A hot flask of soup is always welcome. If you are observing in a remote area, take a mobile phone with you. Red accompanies me everywhere. He loves the night, especially on the moorlands, but even Red gets cold and hungry on a freezing night. If you take your best friend, do look after him/her. During the summer months, especially August, carry insect repellent with you unless you enjoy being eaten alive by midges, and take a flask containing a cool drink. If you have access to a pool, lie in the shallow end intermittently to cool down.

The best position to observe the sky is lying on your back looking directly up. A portable sun lounger or reclining chair is ideal. If you stand staring up at the sky for long periods of time you will give yourself a severe pain in the neck. Set your sun lounger facing the direction you wish to observe, lie back and that's it.

Remember, it takes at least twenty minutes for your eyes to become accustomed to the dark. You will see many things you had not noticed before and be surprised at the number of satellites zipping over. Every little nuance in the night sky will be illuminated to you. After a while, maybe an hour, your mind will drift away and you feel as if you are actually floating among the star fields. You become disembodied and the sensation is quite wonderful. You will know intuitively you are a part of this vast universe and that you belong. The problems of the world evaporate when faced with this immenseness, and it puts your life into perspective. It is a holistic encounter.

The human eye has two types of sensors: rods and cones. Cones function well in bright light, perceive colour and fine detail. Rods are far more sensitive allowing night vision when your pupils are wide open. Rods do not distinguish colour or fine detail and are mostly insensitive to red light. Although rods do not respond to colour they give the sensation of black, white or grey. An important point to note when observing is that rods and cones are not distributed uniformly across the retina. Cones are only found at the centre of the retina (fovea) while rods dominate the periphery. This is the reason you often see 'something' through the corner of your eye and when you look directly at the 'something' it has disappeared. It is also the reason your pupils dilate when dark.

When observing look for shapes, shadows, contrast and movement. Since the centre of your pupil is insensitive at low-level illumination keep looking towards the side. Keep your eyes in motion and do not stare directly at a sighted object. To avoid eye fatigue close your eyes for a few seconds every couple of minutes but do not fall asleep!

Practical Equipment Checklist
A pair of binoculars
A torch or two
A compass
A planisphere or star map

Binoculars

I use a pair of 7 x 50 binoculars, which I bought many years ago. If you do not have a pair of binoculars, just look at the sky with the naked eye. If you are motivated, try and identify individual stars and constellations from your star map and check the sky for local conditions.

A Torch or Two

If you live in an area where street lighting is common, the blackness may come as a shock to you when you observe the sky from a dark observing site, especially if there is no Moon. In the country you will need two torches: a strong torch to light up foot paths leading to your observation site, and a dim torch to use once your eyes are fully accustomed to the darkness. You can lose your night sensitivity in a couple of seconds by switching on a powerful torch. This is why a weak torch, with a red piece of plastic over the beam should be used to help you preserve your 'night sight'. If you are really keen, special astronomical torches based on red Light Emitting Diodes (LEDs) are available.

A Compass

If you travel away from bright city lights and familiar surroundings to a dark location, a magnetic compass is useful (and exciting) for finding north and estimating the 'azimuth' (bearing from North) of the objects you may want to observe. Camping shops sell compasses and many come with a small plastic ruler attached. Magnetic North is a few degrees out from true north.

A Star Chart, Reference Book or Planisphere

Do not carry heavy star charts or giant sky atlases with you. You need to travel light. The only essential heavy item you need to carry is your night picnic or midnight feast! Even if you hate the idea of looking at a star chart, eventually, you will want to identify objects in the sky. I know the sky intimately but I always carry a simple 'planisphere' with me. The advantage of a planisphere over a star chart is you can find which constellations are visible at any time of night and on any date in the year.

The planisphere is a descendant of the astrolabe. A modern planisphere consists of two plastic discs fastened in the middle. The top disc has a scale of hours around the edge, and the bottom disc has a scale of days and months. By rotating the top disc so the hour of the night corresponds to the date, a window will show what stars are visible in the sky at that time and date. Planispheres are calculated for a given geographical latitude. You need a planisphere for latitude of roughly 52 degrees North, which is usable from 57 degrees North down to 48 degrees North, which is OK for the whole of the British Isles.

The Fragile Shroud

All living structures adjust their behaviour according to natural light. Modern societies have the ability to turn night into day by the use of powerful artificial lights. This light creates stress and confusion. If it is not suitably controlled obtrusive light causes serious physiological and ecological problems not only for the present generation but for future generations too.

Light pollution is the sky-glow produced by the scattering of artificial light in gases, dust particles and water droplets of the air. A significant proportion of artificial light ends up in the sky where it does nothing to increase night time safety and security. It wastes not only electricity and large sums of money, but more importantly, the Earth's finite energy resources. Indirectly, this results in emissions of greenhouse gases. Light, whether it keeps you awake at night by shining through a bedroom window (light trespass) or impedes your view of the night sky, is a form of pollution.

Without too much effort light pollution can be substantially reduced without detriment to social lighting objectives. We can help to protect the nocturnal environment, reducing the disturbance of natural habitats of animals, plants and ecological processes, and we can avoid glare that impedes aircraft and ships. Sky-glow brightens the night sky for everyone: you, amateur, professional astronomers and me. It presents a particularly potent threat to professional astronomers. Advances at the frontiers of astronomy require observations of very faint objects studied with large telescopes located at prime observing sites away from sources of air pollution and general sky-glow. Most observations of cosmological interest deal with extremely remote sources: galaxies or quasars at great distances. Their light has travelled for billions of years, sometimes twice the age of the Earth, only to be lost in the glare of our civilisation during the last one thousandth of a second of its journey.

We can minimise light pollution without compromising night time safety and security by:

    i Using night lighting only when necessary; using timers; using the correct amount of light for the need, not overkill.

ii Directing the light downwards where it is needed. The use and effective placement of well-designed fixtures will achieve excellent lighting control. The goal is to use fixtures, which control the light well, minimising glare, light trespass, light pollution and energy usage.

iii Using low-pressure sodium (LPS) light sources whenever possible. This is the best possible light source to minimise adverse effects on astronomical activities. LPS lamps are also the most energy efficient light sources that exist. Areas where LPS is especially good include street lighting, car park lighting, security lighting and any application where colour identification is not critical.

We must do what we can now to protect the night time environment. It is another of the key environmental issues confronting our civilisation and one which merits an increased awareness.

Earth's Atmosphere

The Earth's atmosphere is a thin layer of gases surrounding the Earth. It is composed of seventy-eight per cent nitrogen, twenty-one per cent oxygen, nine-tenths of a per cent argon, point zero three per cent carbon dioxide and trace amounts of other gases. The atmosphere was formed by planetary degassing, a process in which gases like carbon dioxide, water vapour, sulphur dioxide and nitrogen were released from the interior of the Earth through volcanoes and other processes. Life forms on Earth have modified the composition of the atmosphere throughout their evolution. The Earth's atmosphere is about 300 miles thick, but most of the Earth's atmosphere is within ten miles of the Earth's surface.

The Greenhouse Effect and Global Warming

The greenhouse effect is neither new nor necessarily bad. Without the greenhouse effect life would probably not exist on the Earth as we know it. The greenhouse effect is the warming of the Earth's surface from heat trapped in the atmosphere. Solar energy released by the Sun penetrates the Earth's atmosphere. About half of the solar energy reaching the Earth's surface is reflected back into space or absorbed in the upper atmosphere. The other half is absorbed by the Earth's land and water masses. As the Earth absorbs solar radiation it is heated and emits a less intense form of energy but at longer wavelengths. Much of this energy passes unimpeded through the atmosphere. The dominant gases in the atmosphere have no effect on the radiated energy. But some trace gases in the atmosphere such as water vapour and carbon dioxide behave differently. They absorb the longer wavelengths of energy or reflect it back to the surface. Like a blanket these minute concentrations of greenhouse gases trap the radiated energy, converting it to heat.

These trace gases in the atmosphere create roughly the same effect as the glass panes of a greenhouse allowing sunlight to pass through but trapping some of the radiated heat. This accounts for the name 'greenhouse effect'. Without the natural phenomenon of the greenhouse effect, the Earth would be cooler by about 35 degrees Celsius, an icy, uninhabitable planet. Today's concern is that human activity may be tipping the Earth's delicate environmental balance by significantly increasing the build-up of greenhouse gases in the atmosphere and enhancing their insulating effect creating global warming with all its adverse meteorological consequences.

Ozone Layer Depletion

The ozone layer surrounds the earth like an invisible veil between twelve and thirty miles above its surface. Ozone (O_3, three atoms of oxygen) is a naturally occurring gas that is continuously being created and destroyed in a part of the upper atmosphere known as the stratosphere. Ozone also exists in a part of the lower atmosphere called the troposphere, where it is formed as a by-product of fossil fuel combustion. Tropospheric ozone is sometimes referred to as 'bad ozone', because it is a major component of smog in cities. Since tropospheric ozone cannot travel into the stratosphere, it does not affect the ozone layer.

The ozone layer is crucial to life on the surface of the Earth because it protects living organisms from the Sun's harmful ultraviolet radiation. Scientists divide the Sun's ultraviolet, or UV, radiation into three types: UVA, UVB, and UVC. The least harmful is UVA, most of which passes through the ozone layer. The most dangerous type is UVC, which is lethal to humans and is completely blocked by the ozone layer. The ozone layer absorbs ninety-five to ninety-eight per cent of UVB radiation, which is known to cause skin cancer and have other negative effects on humans and the environment. Since depletion of the ozone layer causes an increase in UVB radiation, we are most concerned about the effects of this type.

The natural formation and destruction of ozone molecules are a result of the absorption of UV light. An oxygen molecule (O_2, two atoms of oxygen) struck by UV light is broken into two single atoms of oxygen (O). The single atoms then combine with other oxygen molecules to form ozone. When an ozone molecule absorbs UVB radiation, it dissociates back to a single oxygen atom and an oxygen molecule. The complete reaction is described below.

$$O_2 + UV \text{ light} = O + O$$
$$O + O_2 = O_3$$
$$O_3 + UV \text{ light} = O_2 + O$$

Human activities in the 20th century have caused significant increases in the stratospheric concentrations of ozone depleting chemicals, throwing the natural equilibrium out of balance. Certain synthetic chemicals which include chlorofluorocarbons (CFCs), halons, methyl chloroform, methyl bromide, carbon tetrachloride and HCFCs (CFC substitutes) are largely to blame for the ozone layer erosion. These chemicals are found in a wide variety of consumer products, such as refrigerant coolants, cleaning solvents and fire fighting agents. They are also used in many common industrial processes.

After being used, these 'ozone eaters' escape into the air as gases. They are very stable compounds that do not react with elements in the lower stratosphere. However, once they drift into the stratosphere UV radiation breaks these ozone depleters down and releases chlorine or bromine. The chlorine or bromine then combines with and destroys ozone faster than it can be naturally created. One CFC molecule can destroy 100 000 ozone molecules. We must focus on eliminating our releases of ozone depleting chemicals and allow stratospheric ozone levels to replenish naturally. To illustrate how little ozone there is: if the ozone layer were at sea level and subject to atmospheric pressure it would form a layer around the Earth only one-eighth of an inch in height!

Binoculars & Telescopes

The telescopes used by Galileo to look at the stars were optically no better than many of today's binoculars. An ordinary pair of binoculars makes a good first astronomical instrument. Binoculars are ideal if you are not sure astronomy is for you. They are easy to operate and can be used for other activities: bird watching and hiking for example. Binoculars are relatively inexpensive, convenient to carry and easy to store. You see the image the right way up and in front of you and the large field of view makes it easy to find what you are looking for. A good pair of binoculars gives a much improved view of the sky over naked eye observation, revealing many sights you may think require a telescope: craters and mountains on the Moon, planets and their moons, the brightest asteroids, passing comets, many double and variable stars, countless star clusters, some nebulae and galaxies. Prism binoculars have been made for over a century and manufacturers have discovered and incorporated many improvements.

Binoculars have a two number designation system, such as 6 x 30 or 7 x 50. The first number is the magnifying power. Magnification simply means making larger. To measure magnification we measure how much bigger an object appears than when viewed with the naked eye. Thus 6 x would be an optical instrument with 6 times magnification. The second number is the diameter of the objective lens in millimetres, i.e. the lens at the front of the binoculars. The larger the diameter of the lens, the more light it can gather and so the brighter the image will be. Many people assume the higher magnification the better. However, high magnification narrows the field of view, making it difficult to find the objects you wish to observe. The worst effect of high power binoculars is their magnification of the dancing of the stars when the instrument is hand held and for this reason, 10 power is the maximum recommended for hand held binoculars.

The bigger the objective lens, the brighter the stars appear. Distant astronomical objects are hard to see because they are faint and need lots of aperture. A pair of 7 x 50 collects twice as much light as a pair of 7 x 35 and hence makes everything appear about 0.7 magnitudes brighter. The disadvantage of the 7 x 50 is they are bigger, making them less appropriate for prolonged use. Binoculars are usually centre-focusing. You turn a knob in the centre of the binoculars to focus both eyes at once. The right hand eyepiece is usually individually focusable so you can correct for differences between your eyes. Centre focusing binoculars are convenient for bird watchers whose targets shift from near to far. Astronomers do not really need this feature as everything in the sky is at the same distance as far as focusing is concerned, a long way off, i.e. at 'infinity'.

You could decide to buy 7 x 50, a good all round choice for stargazing. I have a pair. You may find similar looking instruments at greatly varying prices. Do these prices reflect the difference in their quality? A pair costing eleven times more than another will not show eleven times as much. A cheap pair of binoculars may be best for a casual user, but quality is important for astronomical observations. If you are serious about astronomy consider the better makes. Second hand binoculars can be bought relatively cheaply. Second hand shops, pawnshops and newspaper ads are good places to look, but you risk getting stuck with a dud pair.

Field glasses are different from binoculars in that they use the simple telescope principle of a concave and convex lens set at opposite ends of a tube. They are really two simple telescopes placed side by side and have a small field of view that limits their design to low magnification only. They do not use the prismatic system associated with binoculars. Opera glasses are a type of field glasses.

What You Can See Through Your Binoculars

The Moon shows as much detail through binoculars as Galileo saw with his simple telescopes: the mountains, craters, and plains. The first glance through binoculars reveals the major dark areas, the seas or mares. When the Moon is a waxing crescent a couple of days after the New Moon, only Mare Crisium is visible. The terminator, the line dividing day and night moves across the disk to unveil ever more features as the Moon's phase grows to first quarter, gibbous, then full. Night by night more details are revealed: Mare Tranquillitatis, Serenitatis, Imbrium, and finally Oceanus Procellarum. Near the terminator, the slanting sunlight casts long shadows, so here, mountains and valleys stand out prominently.

Mercury can sometimes be located during twilight with the naked eye, but binoculars make it much easier to pick up. The little planet only appears star-like, i.e. featureless.

Venus will show its crescent phase in high-quality binoculars.

Mars looks like a bright orange star.

Jupiter is one of the binocular showpieces of the sky. Its four bright Galilean moons are lined up on each side of the planet in patterns that change every night. The two outer moons of Jupiter: Ganymede and Callisto, are the most easily seen in binoculars. Europa and Io remain hidden in Jupiter's bright glare until you catch them at their greatest distance from the planet. All four are roughly the size of our own Moon or a little larger. Comparing these tiny pinpoints with the full Moon, through binoculars, emphasises how much farther away they are.

Saturn's lone 'binocular' moon Titan is difficult to find. An 8th magnitude speck, it only gets about as far from Saturn as 6th magnitude Europa does from Jupiter. It needs large, high-power binoculars. Saturn's rings, unfortunately, cannot be seen very definitely with magnifications less than about 20x or 30x, so a telescope might be your best bet, if you are a Saturn fan.

Uranus, Neptune, and the half dozen or so asteroids that reach 8th magnitude or brighter look like faint stars. Uranus, Neptune and bright asteroids can be found with binoculars with the aid of the charts.

Deep-Sky Objects

If you already know the constellations with the naked eye, you will discover binoculars show countless new stars in what used to be blank spaces. Sweep from one bright star to another in familiar constellations and get used to finding your way around. If the sky is dark and free of light pollution, a pair of 7 x 50 or 10 x 50 binoculars should show all stars 9th magnitude and brighter and most deep space objects described as 8th magnitude or brighter. As with a telescope, your charts and reference books are crucial to success at this level of observation.

Observing Tips

The biggest problem with binoculars is holding them steady. The constant dancing of the stars prevents you seeing the faintest objects. Lying on your back and resting their weight on the cheekbones below your eyes (zygomatic arch) will reduce the dancing to a wiggle in time with your heartbeat. Many binoculars can be attached to a photographic tripod. This holds them perfectly still for near horizontal viewing but you cannot get underneath a tripod to look up. A number of special binocular mounts for astronomers are available. They are large and expensive but the best work extremely well. A usual way of coping with 'the shakes' is to observe from a sun lounger that has arms. By resting both elbows on the sun lounger's arms and the eyepieces against your face, the dancing is greatly reduced.

You will not be able to set up a tripod over your sun lounger. However, if the binoculars are attached to a tripod or a long piece of two by two timber lying across your lap and sticking out sideways into the air, the image becomes very still. Merely attaching the binoculars to such a large, rigid object is enough to stop the troublesome rapid jittering. With the binoculars held still, their performance will seem to be doubled. Compare the detail visible in solidly mounted 6 x 30 binoculars with hand-held 10 x 50. Rubber eyecups are very good, especially if artificial lights intrude on your observing site.

Magnitude

Stars are subdivided into magnitudes according to their apparent brightness. The lower the number the brighter the star. Any star is about two and half times as bright as the one of the next magnitude. The faintest stars visible to the naked eye are of the sixth magnitude or one-hundredth the brightness of one of first magnitude. On a Moonless night, the total number of stars visible is about 2500. Zero magnitude represents brightness two and half times that of first magnitude. Sirius is -1.47, Venus is -4.4, the Full Moon is -12.5 and the Sun is -26.6 or 444 000 times as bright as the Full Moon.

Binoculars At Night

We measure the effectiveness of binoculars for night use by the 'exit pupil'. The exit pupil is the diameter of the light rays exiting from the eyepiece of a pair of binoculars towards your eye. The exit pupil number is found by dividing the objective lens diameter by the magnification power: 7 x 35 = 5 mm exit pupil, 7 x 50 = 7 mm exit pupil. The pupil is about 7 mm in diameter when fully dilated. If the exit pupil is less than 7 mm the eye is not fully used. Binoculars should be held, aimed straight forward and the eyes turned off centre to avoid using the insensitive centre of the retina. This technique requires practice but it is very effective.

Telescopes

Magnified images of the Moon, Mars, Jupiter or Saturn take your breath away! Regrettably, most of the thousands of astronomical objects visible through a small telescope are not breathtaking sights, even when you know the objects are millions of light years distant. Many people buy a telescope expecting to see super-duper, computer enhanced, deep-space 'pictures' in the eyepiece. You do not! If you are thinking of purchasing a telescope for visual thrills you will soon be disillusioned. A telescope offers a different kind of experience and if you are not really serious about 'observational astronomy' it is best to stick with a good pair of binoculars rather than spend money on a quality instrument. Observing the stars seriously, can mean being outdoors in the dark and trying to detect a very faint, 'hard to find' object. It requires patience, humility and a Zen like calmness. The ecstasy of observational astronomy is in finding and seeing 'invisible' objects that lie far beyond our solar system.

Buying a Telescope

If you are uncertain, ask your local astronomy society for advice. Many members of astronomical societies own their own telescope and will give you advice on price, portability and specialist shops in the area. Indeed, so keen are some members of astronomical societies, they might actually scare you off with their enthusiasm. So be firm with them. Before buying a telescope, ask yourself: are you familiar with the sky? Can you find the Milky Way? Can you name a constellation? Do you know which planets are visible? If you cannot answer these questions, should you be buying a telescope?

If you decide you want a telescope, the first rule is not to rush to your nearest department store. Most department stores do not sell quality telescopes. Their prices are low and so usually are the quality of their telescopes. If all you want to do is look at craters of the Moon, fine. However, if you would like to observe other objects in the night sky you need a good instrument. Avoid telescopes claiming to have a lot of power or magnification. High magnification is not useful because the atmosphere is too unsteady to allow worthwhile observing. Most observing magnifications for a modest telescope are between 50 to 125 powers: 50 x, 125 x. This is more than enough to see craters on the Moon, the rings of Saturn and the moons of Jupiter.

Pay attention to aperture. Aperture refers to the diameter of the lens or the mirror collecting the light. The bigger the lens or mirror the more light can be collected. The more light collected means fainter objects can be seen. There is one thing to bear in mind: the larger the mirror/lens, the larger the telescope which can make it difficult to transport and move. A simple, wiggle free altazimuth mount is better than a flimsy equatorial mount. Look for a telescope using eyepieces with the standard one and a quarter inch diameter barrel. Otherwise, eyepieces may be hard to find or extremely expensive. Do not let the price put you off and if you cannot afford to buy now, save another year until you can afford a suitable instrument.

Taking care of your Instrument.

This advice applies equally to binoculars and telescopes.

i) No satisfactory viewing can be accomplished unless the instrument is firmly supported by a steady stand, even of the simplest construction.

ii) The object glass and the lenses of the eyepiece should be kept clean. Dust may be removed with a clean, camel hairbrush and the lenses then gently wiped with a clean linen handkerchief. Never rub hard.

iii) Do not remove the object lens from its metal cell.

iv) The dew-caps of binoculars and telescopes should always be taken off immediately before observing. If the telescope has no dew-cap, a cardboard or metal cap, blackened inside, should be fitted to replace the lost cap of the object glass when the telescope is not in use.

v) Before bringing the instrument into the house after use, cover the object glass with its cap; otherwise the object glass may become dewed.

vi) If accidentally dewed, the object glass should be gently warmed and then cleaned

vii) Be careful to avoid breathing on the eyepiece when using the telescope.

viii) NEVER, NEVER look at the Sun directly unless a special solar filter has been fitted at the eyepiece (NOT fitted at the object glass).

ix) An image of the Sun may be safely projected onto a smooth white card held a foot or so from the eyepiece and looked at from one side.

Part Four

Beyond The Blue Horizon: Are We Alone?

Life in the Universe

I have never met ET and yet I am confident there are other intelligent beings somewhere in the universe. I am confident because our knowledge of the Earth and the universe suggests so strongly we are not unique and therefore, not alone. The basic materials of life are carbon compounds. These compounds permeate the whole universe. They are everywhere and exist not only on planets, but also in comets, meteors and freely floating giant clouds of gas in space. We know our Sun is just an ordinary star and there are literally billions of Suns in the Milky Way galaxy. We know when stars form, a planetary system also forms. Planetary system formation would follow similar patterns for similar types of star. Small rocky planets like the Earth 'evolve' near a star and giant gas planets, like Jupiter farther out. There must be millions of Earth type planets where life could evolve. I believe enough time has elapsed since the beginning of star formation for countless life forms to have evolved into advanced civilisations.

If we study life on Earth, there are basic characteristics to guide us when we consider life elsewhere in the universe. All forms of life on Earth, no matter how diverse, share common building blocks. All life is made from the same basic units: cells. Every cell is an elaborate structure made up of complex molecules. However, all molecules have one common characteristic: they are made from long chains of the atom carbon. Carbon is the fourth most abundant element in the universe. The cloud of gas that gave birth to the solar system was rich in carbon. On Earth, these simple compounds grew into larger molecules, which eventually came together to produce the first cells. It is from these simple cells, life has evolved into the wide diversity of plants and animals we see around us today.

The Planets

The obvious place to start our search for life is in our own solar system. The solar system however, has turned out to be something of a disappointment regarding intelligent life or any life at all. Not too long ago, the planets seemed to hold a lot of potential but as spacecraft looked closely, hopes were dashed. The planets are either deep frozen or deep fried worlds, uninhabitable gas giants or uninhabitable rocky morsels. The planets are either smothered by toxic atmospheres or are almost totally airless and altogether poor company for a world like Earth, which is teeming with life.

Even Mars has turned out to be a barren, frozen world with a thin atmosphere. The valleys on Mars look as if they once contained rivers, so life may have existed there millions of years ago. Perhaps some living cells might even be preserved in the frozen soil. The famous Martian meteorite (1996) ALH84001 thought to contain fossilised micro bacteria turned out to be as dead as a Dodo. Fortunately, the planets are not the only members of the Sun's family. The solar system is packed with moons, more than five dozen of them, and astronomers are beginning to believe these cosmic offspring may be more remarkable than the parent worlds they orbit. Unlike most of the planets, these moons have oceans, continents and active volcanoes.

Moons

It now seems a moon is the best place to look for extraterrestrial life in the solar system. We are talking 'primitive' life, not intelligent life. In 1979 during the Voyager 1 spacecraft's first encounter with the Jovian moon Io, astronomers began to suspect there might be more to the moons than first met the telescopic eye. While forty-five of the sixty-four moons in the solar system measure less than 300 miles in diameter, most of the others are more than 1200 miles across. Bodies with this kind of bulk are capable of supporting an atmosphere and this is a big plus when you are trying to incubate life. What the moons lacked was the heat needed to get biological chemistry going, or so astronomers thought.

When the first pictures of Io were beamed to Earth, astronomers got a big shock. Rising from Io's face were the unmistakable plumes of up to ten erupting volcanoes. It became clear other bodies in the solar system could be geologically active. Ordinarily, a body the size of Io should have cooled long ago, making volcanoes impossible. But for every orbit the moon makes around Jupiter, it makes several passes of its large, slower orbiting sister moons: Europa, Ganymede and Callisto. Every time Io approaches or passes one of these moons the gravitational tug gives Io a 'ping'. On Earth, the gravity of just one moon is sufficient to cause the oceans to rise and fall in great crashing tides. On Io the gravitational influence of three nearby moons is enough to distort the shape of the world itself, causing it to pulse like a heartbeat. This rhythmic motion churns up internal heat, which in turn stirs up moon-wide volcanoes. These otherworldly eruptions are dramatic.

Jupiter's ice covered moon, Europa has a frosty skin, a planet-wide ice cap floating on top of a global ocean of ordinary water. Brown stains have been spotted on the ice that could conceivably be a mixture of hydrogen cyanide or other life related chemicals. If it is hydrogen cyanide then there are organic chemicals mixed in a sea of water and that is a recipe for life. Tidal heating on Europa may have produced something truly remarkable. The formations photographed from spacecraft are definitely icebergs, though less jagged looking than those found on Earth.

Astronomers do not know why Europan ice and terrestrial ice would not fracture in the same way, but admit they have no experience with the kinds of cracks that would be produced when an entire world is frozen over. The icebergs are small, rising just 300 to 600 ft. above the surrounding ice. Since only ten per cent of an iceberg shows above the water it means these would measure a mile or so from top to bottom, so, therefore would the planet-wide ice crust from which they came. On the scale of a 2000-mile wide moon, that is not much of a crust. No matter how thick the ice is, the waters beneath it must still be liquid, thanks to tidal heating. This is good news for biology. Scientists do not pretend to know how warm a Europan ocean might be but even waters just a degree above freezing would feel very pleasant to organisms that evolved in it.

While Europa may be the solar system's most promising Petri dish, it is by no means the only one. Saturn's moon Titan is larger than both Mercury and Pluto and has an atmosphere sixty per cent denser than the Earth's. Titan's atmosphere forms a sort of photochemical haze, which appears to be full of the stuff of pre-biology. The problem is Titan is cold, with temperatures hovering near -144 degrees C and no signs yet of significant heat to drive chemical reactions. The moon could be awash with organics unable to combine in biologically useful ways. If there is lightning in the Titanian atmosphere it could energise organic molecules.

Jupiter's Io and Neptune's Triton could also prove surprising. Though Io appears largely dehydrated, planetologists do not rule out the possibility of subsurface water, particularly since they think ordinary steam might provide some of the propulsive muscle behind the moon's volcanoes. Triton presents a greater organic hurdle. At -183 degrees C this moon is the coldest known object in the solar system. Nevertheless, it appears heavy with subsurface ice that seems to have been warm enough in the past to flow over the landscape in a lava-like slurry. More tantalising, dark streaks near the poles suggest occasional geysering on the frozen moon may have spouted carbon or some other organic material. These moons make one of the most fascinating cosmic families imaginable.

Cosmic Ancestry

Panspermia is a theory postulating life on Earth was seeded from space and life's evolution to higher forms depends on genetic programs coming from space. Its earliest advocate was the Greek philosopher Anaxagoras but Aristotle's theory of 'spontaneous generation' came to be preferred and adopted for more than two thousand years. In 1864 the French chemist Louis Pasteur announced his great experiment disproving spontaneous generation. In the 1870s, British physicist Lord Kelvin and German physicist Hermann von Helmholtz reinforced Pasteur's theory and argued life could come from space. In the first decade of the twentieth century, Swedish chemist and Nobel laureate Svante Arrhenius theorised bacterial spores propelled through space by light pressure were the seeds of life on Earth.

Careful spectroscopic observation and analysis of light from distant stars has found evidence of traces of organic molecules in the intervening dust. Comets made mostly of water-ice carry bacterial life across galaxies deep within their nucleus that protects it from radiation damage along the way. There is now some agreement that space contains the ingredients of life and this development could be the first hint of a shift away from neo-Darwinian evolution. Mainstream science has not accepted the core theory of modern panspermia that whole cells seeded life on Earth. While accepting the fact life on Earth evolved over the course of about four billion years, the genetic programs for higher evolution cannot be explained by random mutation and recombination among genes for single celled organisms, even over that length of time. The programs must come from somewhere beyond Earth. The theory infers that all of life comes from space.

Gaia theory proposes living structures control the Earth's environment to make it suitable for life. It is hard to imagine how purposeful Gaian processes taking millions of years could be discovered by trial and error. However, Panspermia endorses Gaia theory and proposes Gaian processes are not blindly found and peculiar to Earth, but are pre-existent and universal and life from space brings Gaian processes with it. Gaian processes are necessary for higher forms of life to emerge and succeed on any planet. The union of Gaia within an expanded theory of panspermia is called: Cosmic Ancestry.

Its account of evolution and the origin of life on Earth are profoundly different from the prevailing scientific paradigm. The theory challenges not merely the answers but the questions that are popular today. Cosmic Ancestry implies, that life can only descend from ancestors that were at least as highly evolved as itself. It means there can be no origin of life from non-living matter in the finite past. Without supernatural intervention life must have always existed. Although these conclusions cut across the boundaries between science, philosophy and religion they are grounded in good evidence. The case for Cosmic Ancestry is not yet proven. However, the neo-Darwinian account of the molecular mechanism behind evolution and the origin of life on Earth, the theory taught in schools today, is also not yet proven.

Is Cosmic Ancestry a viable scientific account of evolution and the origin of life on Earth? Only time will tell, but the idea fits well with the ancients' view of the world, especially their fear of and reverence for comets.

Search for Extraterrestrial Intelligence

On August 15th 1977 the 'Big Ear' astronomical radio telescope at Ohio State Observatory in the US tuned in to a hydrogen megahertz frequency. In 1977, telescope data was printed on reams of paper because there were no monitors and no computer memory back up. Professor Ehman, a radio astronomer looked through the evening's data and got the shock of his life. At one point, the voltage peaks jumped off the page. A powerful radio signal had been intercepted by the telescope. The signal lasted thirty-seven seconds and Professor Ehman scribbled 'WOW!' in the margin of the printout. To this day, the burst of radio noise remains the $64 000 question and is known as the WOW signal. The signal could not be stored electronically. In 1977 computers, even at Ohio State Observatory were still in the Stone Age. The Ohio computer had a measly 32K RAM and a hard disc of one megabyte. Today's home PCs have as standard 256MB RAM and 40 Gigabyte hard disc!

Astronomers are now willing to accept the 'WOW' signal may have come from an advanced alien civilisation. The unmodulated blast of radio noise appears to contain no message. Each channel on the Big Ear receiver spanned ten kilohertz, which could easily encompass a carrier (containing a message) and sidebands. Ohio were not able to distinguish between the two. According to records, the nearest star in the direction of Big Ear was 220 light years away. If the transmission dish for this signal were as big as today's largest radio telescope it would require a two-gigawatt transmitter. Since 1977 astronomers have performed over 100 studies of the same region of the sky but the signal has never been repeated. It is not surprising as Big Ear sees only about a millionth of the sky at a time. So the chance of an alignment between the transmitting and receiving beacon is extremely unlikely. After twenty-five years WOW remains the only intercepted signal from ET. Or, the WOW signal is a previously undiscovered astrophysical phenomenon. The former remains the most probable!

SETI

Even though no extraterrestrial life forms have yet been discovered, astronomers believe the universe is teeming with intelligent life. Our solar system may contain primitive life forms but to discover intelligent life we have to look towards the stars. Given the level of 20th century technology, the only way we could look was to listen. In the 21st century, laser and photometer systems will send messages to and hopefully receive messages from ET. The Search for Extraterrestrial Intelligence (SETI) set up over forty years ago has been panning the skies with large Earth based radio telescopes listening for ET signals (Professor Ehman at Big Ear was working on a SETI project in 1977).

The only 'ET' transmissions SETI had a chance of detecting in the 20th century were 'radio beacons'. A radio beacon is a strong signal deliberately designed to advertise your presence to anyone who may be listening. Search projects undertaken were too weak to pick up any radio chatter from ET's internal traffic. Internal traffic refers to television and radio broadcasts and point-to-point radio communications. Judging from trends in our own radio technology there is every reason to suppose the more advanced an alien civilisation, the less recognisable their internal communications become from a distance. Optical-fibre, hard-wire, directional satellite transmission and digital systems all reduce radio noise that previously may have escaped into space.

You can search for ET too: SETI@home

Over one million people around the world are now participating in one of the most ambitious experiments undertaken in the search for extraterrestrial intelligence, by using their PCs at home to process radio telescope data that might contain a signal from 'ET'. Sifting through huge volumes of radio data takes massive computing power. Even the powerful super computers specially designed for SETI projects cannot handle all the data. You can sign up and may even be the one who discovers the first extraterrestrial signal. Simply connect to the internet and call SETI@home.

The SETI@home network is really the world's largest supercomputer. SETI@home's goal is to analyse recorded data, about 100 million work units, each one of which involves 175 billion operations on someone's PC. SETI@home has now accumulated more than 100 000 years of computer time, more than any other computing project in history, and has recorded over eighty-five million 'candidate signals' in their database.

Optical SETI

Each of the SETI search projects represents a major advance over previous projects, the latest one (Alien Telescope Array) being billions of times more powerful than the first project, Ozma of 1960. Using existing optical telescopes with laser and photometer facilities, optical SETI can search for light and infrared signals from an advanced civilisation. We can also send signals. A powerful laser could direct a short burst of beacon signals to perhaps a million stars each day. The signals could be detected across 1000 light years by today's optical telescopes. If ET uses a somewhat bigger laser the signals could be detected by an amateur telescope equipped with a pair of low cost, high-speed photo-multipliers. This latest project will study 2500 mostly Sun-like stars as well as globular clusters and galaxies.

Is ET Already Here?

The above ET search is quite irrelevant to millions of people across the world who have observed at a distance, witnessed at close quarters or have already made contact with ET. Ninety-eight per cent of all Unidentified Flying Objects UFOs can be accounted for by logical explanations: freak meteorological conditions, an exceptionally bright meteor, planetary conjunctions and even the earth lights that glow in the sky around the time of an earthquake. The remaining two per cent cannot. Much confusion exists in the area of UFOlogy because serious investigation carried out by private organisations is marginalised and government intelligence gathering organisations keep their information secret. The subject also attracts the interest of more than a few crackpots!

However, thousands of UFO sightings have been made by people not usually given to mindless speculation. They began in 1933 when ghost aircraft appeared over Scandinavia and not, as is commonly believed in the United States. Currently, triangular shaped craft of unknown origin, termed Flying Triangles (FTs) are observed worldwide.

Leading researcher Omar Fowler of the Phenomenon Research Association believes there to be a persistent occurrence around planet Earth which manifests itself in a very odd way and which seems to indicate a degree of intelligence. The experience of the military is that it flickers in and out, it appears on radar then disappears. UFOs have come near to causing aircraft accidents though they have not been directly blamed for any accident. Hardheaded civilian airline pilots are extremely reluctant to report sightings. But it would be intellectual cowardice to argue away the hard core of these UFO reports. If the experts are right and UFO sightings continue at their present rate one thing seems conceivable, sooner or later the 'near miss' may become a collision. Only then perhaps will we begin to understand a phenomenon once dismissed as fantasy and now recognised as one of the greatest mysteries of our time. Until then, we can only wait and wonder.

The Drake Equation

How can we estimate the number of technological civilisations that might exist among the stars? While working as a radio astronomer at the National Radio Astronomy Observatory in Green Bank, West Virginia, Dr. Frank Drake conceived an approach to bind the terms involved in estimating the number of technological civilisations that may exist in our galaxy. The Drake Equation, as it has come to be known, was first presented by Drake in 1961 and identifies specific factors thought to play a role in the development of such civilisations. Although there is no unique solution to this equation, it is a generally accepted tool used by the scientific community to examine these factors.

$$N = R_* \times f_p \times n_e \times f_l \times f_i \times f_c \times L$$

N = The number of communicative civilisations. The number of civilisations in the Milky Way Galaxy whose radio emissions are detectable.

R_* = The rate of formation of suitable stars. The rate of formation of stars with a large enough habitable zone and long enough lifetime to be suitable for the development of intelligent life.

f_p = The fraction of those stars with planets. The fraction of Sun-like stars with planets is currently unknown, but evidence indicates that planetary systems may be common for stars like the Sun.

n_e = The number of Earth type planets per planetary system. All stars have a habitable zone where a planet would be able to maintain a temperature that would allow liquid water. A planet in the habitable zone could have the basic conditions for life as we know it.

f_l = The fraction of those planets where life develops. Although a planet orbits in the habitable zone of a suitable star, other factors are necessary for life to arise. Thus, only a fraction of suitable planets will actually develop life.

f_i = The fraction of life sites where intelligence develops. Life on Earth began over three and a half billion years ago. Intelligence took a long time to develop. On other life-bearing planets it may happen faster, it may take longer, or it may not develop at all.

f_c = The fraction of planets where technology develops. The fraction of planets with intelligent life that develop technological civilisations, i.e., technology that releases detectable signs of their existence into space.

L = The Lifetime of communicating civilisations. The length of time such civilisations release detectable signals into space.

Enigmas

Why is it dark at night?

This may at first appear to be a silly question. We all know it goes dark at night because the Sun sets. However, if there are an infinite number of stars in the universe and the universe is infinitely large we should see stars crammed into every niche in the sky. If a small telescope shows two stars in a given field of view, a more powerful telescope should reveal more stars filling the space between them. A still more powerful telescope should find stars filling the space between them and so on until all we see are stars and no sky at all. The night sky should be a blinding sheet of light, as bright as the surface of the Sun. Yet at night, the sky is dark.

The answer to this riddle was not solved until the early twentieth century when Edwin Hubble discovered the expansion of the universe. The quest to find an answer began in 1826 when Wilhelm Olbers wrote a little paper posing one of the most unsettling questions of scientific theory. Why, he asked, is the sky dark at night? Throughout the eighteenth and nineteenth centuries the universe was presumed to be infinite. This view avoided the dilemma of how a three dimensional universe could be finite. If the universe came to an end, what lay beyond? In 1692 Newton wrote, if the number of stars in the universe were finite their combined gravity would pull them together and they would fall down into the middle of space, and there compose one great spherical mass. The alternative to this rather sad state of affairs was an infinite universe peppered with an infinite number of stars. If matter was evenly sprinkled throughout an infinite space it could never convene into one mass. This satisfied everyone until Olbers asked: why is it dark at night?

Prior to Olbers, it had been assumed most of the infinite stars were invisible simply because they were too far away to be seen from Earth. The apparent brightness of a star diminishes by the square of its distance, so if one star is 100 light years distant and another identical star is 200 light years distant, the second star will appear one quarter as bright as the first. Olbers examined the problem critically and found that contrary to what had been assumed before, the cumulative brightness of an infinite number of stars should overwhelm the dimming effect of their distance. Olbers realised if we do live in a static, infinite universe, the night sky should be brilliantly bright. The puzzle is known as 'Olbers' Paradox'.

Olbers considered and rejected two solutions. One was to assert that the stars far away from the Sun were, for some reason, intrinsically dimmer. The second was to say the universe is infinite but the number of stars was not. Perhaps the cosmos was composed of the Milky Way, empty space and nothing else. Olbers finally decided interstellar dust absorbed the light from distant stars. This was an astute conjecture but it turned out to be insignificant. Given infinite time, starlight would heat up interstellar dust and gas until it glowed and the universe would be as bright as the Sun. (The laws of Thermodynamics devised after Olbers' death made that clear and renewed the paradox.)

Why the night sky is dark was resolved when Hubble discovered the expansion of the universe. The sky is dark because the universe is expanding, and the universe does not collapse because it is expanding. To answer Olbers' paradox, the sky is not dazzlingly bright because the universe is using its energy to expand. The remote galaxies discard so much of their light into the red shift, so much of their energy is thinned out over increasing space and time that the sky looks dark. It is amazing that so familiar a sight as the dark sky of night results from so magnificent a source as the motions of distant galaxies.

Confused by Big Numbers

Everyone gets confused by big numbers and the number: one billion creates big confusion. Until recently, the UK took one billion to mean a million million, a '1' followed by twelve zeroes. In the US, one billion is taken as one thousand million, a '1' followed by nine zeroes. The need for a common meaning for the word has caused the UK to adopt the US system and in all fields the American usage now prevails: one billion is one thousand million, a '1' followed by nine zeroes.

The system of naming large powers of ten started in the 1480s. The system devised was based on powers of a million and named using a set of prefixes derived from the Latin: bi, tri, quadr, quint, and so on, plus the suffix 'illion' derived from million. So a trillion was the third power of a million, a '1' followed by eighteen zeroes. Over the following century this system was adopted in much of continental Europe and in Britain.

Then something strange happened. French speakers changed the system to one in which the multiples were not of a million but of a thousand. It was in the middle of the 17th century the erroneous custom of dividing series of figures above a million into groups of three, and calling a thousand million a billion, and a thousand billions a trillion, and so on. It was an entire perversion of the nomenclature. The problem was, the same words were used in both systems, which led inevitably to confusion. The table below shows how the two systems relate. The numbers indicate the power of ten involved in each case, so that '9' means ten to the power of nine, or a '1' followed by nine zeroes. All the prefixes are derived from Latin roots.

Number-word	Millions-system No of zeros	Thousands-system No of zeros
Million	6	6
Billion	12	9
Trillion	18	12
Quadrillion	24	15
Quintillion	30	18
Sextillion	36	21
Septillion	24	42
Octillion	48	27
Nonillion	54	30
Decillion	60	33
Undecillion	66	36
Duodecillion	72	39
Tredecillion	78	42
Quattuordecillion	84	45
Quindecillion	90	48
Sexdecillion	96	51

The separation between the millions system and the thousands system increases rapidly as you move upwards.

Some countries followed the new French practice while others stayed with the older one. In particular, the young United States took over the revised French system but Britain did not. Which system is used in each country depends, in part, on the point in history at which they came under the influence of one or other European country.

Systeme International

Large numbers usually only appear in scientific or technical journals where scientific notation is appropriate, or in which the standard set of prefixes agreed under the Systeme International (SI) system can be used. These Systeme International (SI) number prefixes go up in multiples of a thousand but, being artificially constructed, do not conflict with the other two systems:

SI prefix	No of zeros	derivation
kilo	3	From the Greek for 'thousand'.
mega	6	From the Greek for 'large; great'.
giga	9	From the Greek for 'giant'.
tera	12	From the Greek for 'monster'.
peta	15	An invented word based on the Greek prefix penta.
exa	18	Derived from the Greek prefix hexa (deleting the first letter).
zetta	21	Adapted from the Italian setta, 'seven'.
yotta	24	Similarly from the Italian otto, 'eight'.

The smaller number prefixes are regularly used in technical contexts. Computing has started to speak of terabytes and to theorise about the need for petabyte levels of storage. They have had little or no impact on the language at large, though 'mega' has taken on a fashionable role as a superlative of 'super' in words like 'megastar'. It is primarily derived from the much older sense of 'large', as in words like 'megalith', (large stone). There are signs we may see 'giga' following it as linguistic inflation continues. Many theme parks around the world are to be called Giga Worlds because according to their promoters, 'Mega' is far too modest a term. I remember supermarkets becoming hypermarkets, then megastores. The gigastores may come next although internet shopping may put a stop to that!

Past, Present & Future

One Billion equals one thousand million
One Trillion equals one thousand billion
One Quadrillion equals one thousand trillion
One Sexdecillion equals one thousand, trillion, trillion, trillion, trillion

Our universe is just a newborn baby. By human and geological standards, fifteen billion years sounds a long time but given the ultimate lifetime of our universe, it is just a fraction of a second. Realising the universe will end, no matter how far in the distant future, is rather shocking. Another blow to the human ego is that at this stage in the evolution of the universe, too little time has passed for many of the more interesting possibilities to occur. I am not saying we live in a boring epoch but the best (cosmologically) is yet to come! As the future unfolds the universe will change dramatically. The stars and galaxies so familiar to us and which define our present epoch will give way to a universe of bizarre frozen stars, evaporating black holes and lone atoms the size of the present day observable universe.

One and a quarter billion years into the future, the Sun will heat up and irradiate all life on Earth. Over the next seven billion years, the Sun will become a fully fledged red giant star and in a few hundred million years more, will exhaust its nuclear fuel, shed its outer layers, become a white dwarf star and begin a slow fade into total blackness. If this were not bad enough, eventually all the stars in the universe will fade when the material from which they are formed becomes depleted. No stars will form and the universe will become dark, cold and empty.

The theory of how the universe was created is now universally agreed upon and is known as the Big Bang. Big Bang theory is overwhelmingly successful in accounting for the properties of our universe, in particular: expansion, the cosmic microwave background radiation and the cosmic chemical abundances, especially the light elements that make up almost all ordinary matter. There are three scenarios of the fate of the universe but its destiny is built in from the start: its density.

i A closed universe: is destined to collapse in on itself
ii An open universe: will expand forever
iii A flat universe: will expand forever but at an ever slower rate approaching, but never quite reaching a standstill. (A balance between the 'open' and 'closed'.)

The final demise of the universe depends on its overall density, a value cosmologists call Omega-nought. A flat universe is defined as Omega having a value of '1'. If Omega has a value greater than '1' even by the smallest amount, the universe contains enough mass/energy for its own gravity to halt expansion and pull everything back together in a 'Big Crunch'. If Omega has a value of less than '1' the universe is expanding faster than its own escape velocity and will continue flying apart forever. Current estimates put the value of Omega at '0.2' which is well below the critical value '1'. The universe will expand forever and have access to an infinite amount of time.

Genesis

No one really knows what happened before Big Bang but quantum cosmology has a theory. The story of our universe may sound a little bizarre and if you have difficulty grasping the concepts it doesn't really matter, and you are not alone. Just get a feel for the instantaneously short time spans and the enormously long time spans. In the beginning, there were many Big Bangs spawning eternally from underlying space-time. Each Big Bang universe sprouts and becomes detached from the under-layer that gave birth to it. The baby universe is self-contained and disconnects from all other universes. This event occurred fifteen billion years ago and took only one hundred, million, trillion, trillion, trillionths of a second.

Ten trillionths of a second later, very high-energy quantum fields were driving a greatly accelerated expansion of space (the inflationary era). These fields produced small density fluctuations in the tiny universe. These slight variations survived as space expanded, becoming the seeds of the galaxies and larger structures of the universe we see today. After ten million, trillion, trillionths of a second, inflation ended and the universe expanded at a more moderate pace.

Radiation Epoch

During the first second of its existence, the universe contained almost nothing but a smooth, dense sea of radiation. Complex particle interactions set up a tiny imbalance of ordinary matter over antimatter. The antimatter and almost all of the ordinary matter annihilated each other, leaving behind the small residue of excess material that makes up the universe we know today. By the age of a few minutes, the cooling universe had synthesised the nuclei of light elements, including hydrogen, helium and lithium. The familiar laws of nuclear physics can be applied to the temperatures, pressures and densities that prevailed during this period in the standard Big Bang model. Calculations of the exact composition of this elemental soup, match what is observed in the oldest matter in the universe today. This sub era is called 'recombination'.

The next major change occurred at age 300 000 years when the universe had cooled enough to allow whole atoms to form and survive for the first time. Previously the temperature was so hot that if an electron joined with a proton to form an atom it would quickly be knocked free again. This event is very important because for the first time it rendered the universe transparent to its own radiation. Before this, the universe was opaque and the radiation interacted continuously with particles of matter. Hydrogen gas is transparent so radiation started to fly free. It has been in free flight ever since. The microwave background radiation observed today is the radiation that broke free during the recombination era.

Stellar Epoch

This is the epoch in which we live. It began one million years after creation and will end around one hundred thousand billion years from now. During this epoch most of the energy in the universe is generated from nuclear fusion in ordinary stars. The first galaxies began to appear during the first billion years. Within galaxies, star formation commenced at a furious rate. Many young galaxies also experienced violent events in connection with their central black hole cores. The black holes ripped apart in-falling stars and surrounded themselves with orbiting discs of hot gas. Eventually, most of these active galaxies and quasars died down. Our Sun and the solar system formed around four and a half billion years ago, after the Milky Way had already existed for a comparable amount of time. Galaxies collided and merged, though these events had little effect on individual stars within the galaxies involved. The Milky Way will interact with the Great Galaxy in Andromeda in about six billion years time. Even if they do not merge on this passing, their fate is sealed. The two galaxies are gravitationally bound and it is only a matter of time before they merge and settle into one large super-galaxy.

A similar fate lies in store for many galaxies. Over the next few thousand billion years, galaxies will coalesce and give way to large amorphous galactic systems. As the stellar epoch continues, a key role will fall to the humble red dwarf stars. Though they have only half the mass of the Sun they are so numerous that their combined mass easily exceeds that of all other stars. The red dwarfs are true misers when it comes to fusing their hydrogen with helium. They hoard their nuclear fuel, so most of them will still be shining several trillion years from now when all the larger stars have burned out.

The long-term evolution of red dwarf stars is different from heavier stars like the Sun. Instead of swelling up and becoming red giants, the dimmer stars will very gradually heat up, enjoying a relatively brief 'high luminosity' phase at the end of their life. A red dwarf will burn at twenty per cent the brightness of the Sun for six billion years. Given the example of the Earth, this phase allows enough time for life to evolve on any appropriate planet. If we could be transported to such a future planet we might find a passable likeness of our Earth under a pleasant sun, but with a black and virtually starless sky. Eventually, even the smallest red dwarfs will burn out. The smallest, dimmest stars will survive for another ten trillion years. As the stellar epoch winds down, the rate of star formation decreases. By 100 trillion years, all reserves of hydrogen will be depleted and normal star formation will shut down forever. The stars will stop shining.

Degenerative Epoch

Most of the mass in the universe will be locked away inside degenerate stellar objects. 'Degeneracy' refers to a particular quantum mechanical state. Degenerate remains include: cold brown dwarfs, white dwarfs and neutron stars. Black holes will also contain some degenerate matter. During the degenerative epoch the universe will be cold and black. Essentially, no radiation from any source will light the eternal night, warm the long frozen planets or endow galaxies with the glow they have today. The cosmic temperature will be a fraction of a degree above absolute zero.

Chance encounters will shift the galactic orbits of dead stars and strip planets, which will subsequently fly free. By ten billion, trillion years, most of the dark stellar objects will be ejected from galaxies to drift through intergalactic space, which would now be a very large realm indeed. A small minority of the more massive dead stars will be accreted by black holes at galactic centres. Black holes will continue to grow as they swallow up stray mass. A rare beacon of light energy will emerge when two brown dwarfs collide to form a low mass star. This smallest of red dwarf stars will live for trillions of years and on average, 100 of these stars will be shining dimly in a galaxy the size of our Milky Way. They will shine with a total luminosity of less than today's Sun. Every trillion years or so, a galaxy will experience the long flare of a supernova explosion as two 'relatively' massive white dwarf stars collide and merge. They will be incredibly spectacular against the dark background of a dying and depleted galaxy. Stellar collisions will continue until each galaxy has ejected all of its stars.

The effects of gravitational radiation become significant at ten trillion, trillion years and this dissipative process causes orbits of every kind to lose energy and decay. Weakly interactive massive particles (dark matter postulated by physicists) will be swept up by the dark white dwarf stars. The dark matter will annihilate itself and provide a source of energy. This annihilation of dark matter will replace nuclear energy and become the universe's dominant energy mechanism. By one million, trillion, trillion years, the supply of weakly interactive massive particles will be depleted and the universe will consist of white dwarfs, brown dwarfs and dead widely scattered planets.

'Grand unified' theories predict protons have a finite lifetime. The length is uncertain at this time but it is in the order of ten trillion, trillion, trillion years. Proton decay marks the final phase of the degenerative epoch. The energy stored in white dwarfs, neutron stars and other objects will dissipate as protons decay into positrons, neutrinos, pions and gamma rays. As protons decay and eradicate all matter, the universe will become even darker and emptier.

Black Hole Epoch

The only stellar mass objects remaining in this epoch are black holes. As white dwarfs evaporate, black holes slowly sweep up material and grow larger. Even black holes do not last forever and eventually they evaporate through a slow quantum mechanical process known as Hawking radiation. Black holes are not absolutely black. Their surface glows by emitting a thermal spectrum of photons. A black hole with a mass of the Milky Way will take two Sexdecillion years to evaporate. The black hole epoch is over when even the largest black holes are gone, four Sexdecillion years from now.

Dark Epoch

The universe is now empty of everything from protons to black holes. Only the sparse waste products from the previous epochs remain: photons, a few neutrinos, electrons, positrons and all are inconceivably far apart. The expanse of space between particles is utterly incomprehensible. Electrons and positrons drifting through space can encounter one another's influence and form a positronium atom, an electron and a positron orbiting each other. Their orbit is larger in size than the entire observable universe today! The electron and positron will spiral in and annihilate each other over an enormously long time scale. These events occasionally produce a photon of ever decreasing energies as the universe inexorably expands, until nothing, absolutely nothing is left!

Part Five

The Blue Details: Systems & Ciphers

The Calendar

We need to keep track of time and complex calendars were developed early in human history. The word calendar originates from the Roman term for the beginning of the month. In agricultural societies the seasonal cycle of the Sun was crucial, but for shorter periods the lunar cycle proved useful. The year does not contain a whole number of days or months and the mean interval between successive vernal equinoxes is 365.2424 days, about eleven minutes less than 365.25 days. The synodic period of the Moon, the time between successive Full Moons or New Moons is about twenty-nine and a half days and thus twelve months consist of about 354 days. Constructing a calendar incorporating both the movements of the Sun and Moon is not a simple task.

The Egyptian calendar provided the simplest solution. The year was made up of twelve months of thirty days each and five days were added at the end. Since this meant an error of about one quarter of a day per year, the starting date of the year slowly drifted forward with respect to the seasons until after 1460 years it returned to where it started. The rising of the Nile, the crucial event in the Egyptian agricultural cycle was predicted by the helical rising of Sirius, the brightest star in the heavens.

Cultures in the ancient Near East relied on a calendar in which months had alternating lengths of twenty-nine and thirty days and added a month about every third year. In ancient Israel an extra month of twenty-nine days every third year, after the sixth month, was added (Adar). But these twenty-nine days would not make up entirely for the deficit of 3 x 11.25 days and in some years, two extra months had to be added. The Greek city-states added months haphazardly as needed and no consistent system of intercalation was ever developed.

Development

The most sophisticated system of keeping the motions of both the Sun and Moon harnessed in a single calendar was developed in Mesopotamia. By the Persian period, the system incorporated the Metonic cycle (after the Greek astronomer Meton) around 425 BC in which the following relationship is used: nineteen solar years contain 6939.75 days; 110 months of twenty-nine days plus 125 months of thirty days add up to 6940 days. Nineteen years contained 235 months and starting in 499 BC. The calendar in that part of the world was regulated on a cycle of intercalating seven extra months in nineteen years. After a few irregularities starting in 384 BC, this scheme was rigorously adhered to through the Greek and Roman conquests until 75 AD.

The Greeks divided the month into three periods of ten days, but a division of seven days was older and more common in the Near East. The names we assign to the days have their origin in the division of the day into twenty-four hours, which originated in Egypt. In the Hellenistic period 300 BC to 100 BC it became common to assign a ruling planet including the Sun and Moon to each hour of the day, similar to the Meg Chinese Moon signs.

The common order of the wandering heavenly bodies was Saturn, Jupiter, Mars, Sun, Venus, Mercury and the Moon. The first hour of the first day was assigned to the Sun, the second to Venus, the third to Mercury, repeating the cycle in the order given above. The twenty-fourth hour was thus assigned to Mercury and the first hour of the second day to the Moon. Naming the days after the planets that rule their first hours, we arrive at the sequence Sun's day, Moon's day, Mars's day, Mercury's day, Jupiter's day, Venus's day, Saturn's day. The English variations on these names are due to substituting Nordic or Saxon gods for some of the Roman names: Tiw for Mars, Wotan for Mercury, Thor for Jupiter, and Frigg for Venus.

The division of the hour into minutes and seconds is derived from the sexagesimal system of the Mesopotamians. The division of the day into twenty-four hours originated with the Egyptians while the seven-day week originated in the ancient Near East, the names deriving from a Greek convention developed during the Hellenistic period. Our calendar is based on the motion of the Sun alone but our various festival dates are based on a combination of the motions of the Sun and Moon. The ancient Roman year (of ten months) commenced with March, as is indicated by the names September, October, November, and December, which the last four months still retain. July and August were anciently denominated Quintillis and Sextillis, their present names having been bestowed as a compliment to Julius Caesar and Augustus.

In the reign of Numa two months were added to the year, January at the beginning and February at the end, and this arrangement continued till the year 452 BC when the Decemvirs changed the order of the months and placed February after January. The months now consisted of twenty-nine and thirty days alternately to correspond with the synodic revolution of the

Moon, so the year contained 354 days. A day was added to make the number odd which was considered more fortunate and the year consisted of 355 days. This differed from the solar year by ten days and a fraction and to restore the coincidence, Numa ordered an additional or intercalary month to be inserted every second year between the 23rd and 24th of February, consisting of twenty-two and twenty three days alternately, so four years constituted 1465 days and the mean length of the year was consequently 366.25 days. The additional month was called Mercedinus or Mercedonius.

According to the above arrangement, the year was too long by one day, which rendered another correction necessary. As the error amounted to twenty-four days in as many years it was ordered that every third period of eight years should contain only three of those months, consisting of twenty-two days each. The mean length of the year was reduced to 365.25 days. It does not appear the length of the intercalary month was regulated by any certain principle, for a discretionary power was left with the pontiffs, to whom the care of the calendar was committed.

Their power was quickly abused to serve political objectives, and the calendar consequently thrown into confusion. By giving a greater or lesser number of days to the intercalary month the pontiffs were enabled to prolong the term of a magistracy or hasten the annual elections; and so little care had been taken to regulate the year. At the time of Julius Caesar the civil equinox differed from the astronomical one by three months, the winter months were carried back into autumn and the autumnal months into summer.

Julian Calendar

In order to put an end to the disorder arising from the negligence or ignorance of the pontiffs, Julius Caesar abolished the use of the lunar year and the intercalary month and regulated the civil year entirely by the Sun. He fixed the mean length of the year at 365.25 days, and decreed every fourth year should have 366 days, the other years each having 365. In order to restore the vernal equinox to March 25th he ordered two extraordinary months to be inserted between November and December in the current year, the first to consist of thirty-three and the second of thirty four days. The intercalary month of twenty-three days fell into the year so the ancient year of 355 days received an augmentation of ninety days. This was called the 'last year of confusion'. The first

Julian year commenced on January 1st on the 46th year before the birth of Christ, and the 708th year from the founding of the city of Rome.

In the distribution of the days through the months, Caesar adopted a simpler arrangement, which has since prevailed. He ordered the first, third, fifth, seventh, ninth and eleventh months, that is January, March, May, July, September and November, should each have thirty-one days, and the other months thirty, excepting February, which in common years should have only twenty-nine days, but every fourth year, thirty days. This order was interrupted to gratify the vanity of Augustus, by giving the month bearing his name as many days as July, which was named after the first Caesar. A day was accordingly taken from February and given to August and in order that three months of thirty-one days might not come together, September and November were reduced to thirty days, and thirty-one given to October and December. For so frivolous a reason was the regulation of Caesar forsaken, and a careless arrangement introduced. The additional day which occurred every fourth year was given to February, as being the shortest month, and was inserted in the calendar between the 24th and 25th day.

Although the Julian method of intercalation is perhaps the most convenient that could be adopted, it extends the year by eleven minutes fourteen seconds. It could not, without correction answer the purpose for which it was devised, namely, that of preserving the same interval of time between the commencement of the year and the equinox. Hipparchus, 125 BC, observed that the excess of 365.25 days above a true solar year would amount to a day in 300 years. The real error is more than double this, and amounts to a day in 128 years; but in the time of Caesar the length of the year was an astronomical element not very well determined. In the course of a few centuries, the equinox retrograded towards the beginning of the year. When the Julian calendar was introduced, the equinox fell on March 25th. At the time of the Council of Nicaea, which was held in 325 AD, it fell on March 21st.

Gregorian Calendar

The Julian Calendar was naturally adopted by the successor of the Roman Empire in Christian Europe with the Papacy at its head. By about 700 AD it had become customary to count years from the starting point of the birth of Christ, later corrected by

Johannes Kepler to 4 BC. But the equinox kept slipping backwards on the calendar one full day every 130 years. By 1500 the vernal equinox fell on March 10th and the autumnal equinox on September 13th. The most important feast day on the Christian calendar is Easter. In the New Testament, Christ's crucifixion occurred in the week of Passover. On the Jewish calendar Passover was celebrated at the Full Moon of the first month (Nissan) of spring.

In developing their own calendar, 4th century AD, Christians put Easter on the first Sunday after the first Full Moon after the spring equinox. If the equinox was wrong, then Easter was celebrated on the wrong day. Most other Christian observances, e.g. the beginning of Lent, are reckoned backwards or forward from the date of Easter. An error in the equinox introduced numerous errors in the entire religious calendar. After the unification of the Papacy in Rome in the fifteenth century, Popes began to consider calendar reform. After several false starts, a commission under the leadership of the Jesuit mathematician and astronomer Christoph Clavius (1537 to 1612) succeeded. In 1582 Pope Gregory XIII ordered ten days to be dropped from October thus restoring the vernal equinox at least to around March 20th, close to what it had been at the time of the Council of Nicaea. In order to correct for the loss of one day every 130 years, the new calendar dropped three leap years every 400 years. Henceforth, century years were leap years only if divisible by 400. Hence, 1600, 2000 and 2400 are leap years.

The new calendar proclaimed from Rome was adopted immediately in Catholic countries. Protestant countries followed more slowly. Protestant regions in Germany and the northern Netherlands adopted the calendar within decades. The English retained the Julian Calendar. Moreover, other countries began the New Year uniformly on January 1st, while the English began it on March 25th, an older custom. The date February 11th 1672 in England was February 21st 1673 on the Continent. After 1700 in which the Julian Calendar had a leap year but the Gregorian did not, the difference was eleven days.

The English and their American colonies finally adopted the Gregorian Calendar in the middle of the eighteenth century. China was the last country to conform to the Gregorian calendar in 1949. However, the era of a world wide uniform calendar is already part of history. Iran returned to the traditional Mohammedan Moon calendar in 1979 after removal of the Shah.

The Gregorian Calendar is useless for astronomy and for the purpose of calculating positions backward in time. For such calculations astronomers use the Julian Date.

The Julian Date

The Gregorian calendar has months with thirty-one days, thirty days, and the number of days in February changes almost every four years. This complicated date system we learned at a young age and easily assimilated, is a difficult system for astronomical computing, and so astronomers adopted the Julian date. A Julian date is defined as the continuous count of days from January 1st 4713 BC Greenwich Mean Noon (equal to zero hours Universal Time). The fraction of each day is represented as a decimal number. Hence noon Greenwich Mean Time (GMT) on January 2nd 4713 BC would have Julian date 1.00000 and 6.00 pm GMT on the same day would have Julian date 1.25000.

Joseph Justus Scaliger is credited with developing the concept of the Julian date in 1583 and naming it in honour of his father Julius Caesar Scaliger. However, it was the astronomer John F. Herschel who turned Scaliger's idea into a complete time system rather than a method of relating years. In 1849 Herschel published 'Outlines of Astronomy' and explained the idea of extending Scaliger's concept to days. The system is similar to the one used in the popular television series 'Star Trek'. The Captain of the Starship Enterprise opens his log and enters the date: 'Captain's log, stardate: 46271.5'.

The Sun's Family

Mercury

Mercury is the closest planet to the Sun. This small, rocky world has almost no atmosphere and a very elliptical orbit generating a huge range in temperature. Mercury's surface ranges in temperature from -168 degrees C to 427 degrees C. Mercury is so close to the Sun it is very hard to see except near sunrise or sunset. Mercury is heavily cratered and its surface is similar to the surface of the Earth's Moon. Mercury does have a magnetic field generated by a partly liquid iron core. Mercury is 3031 miles in diameter and is the second smallest planet in our Solar System after Pluto. Mercury is a bit over one third of the diameter of the Earth and is slightly larger than the Earth's Moon. The gravity on Mercury is thirty-eight per cent of the gravity on Earth. A 100-pound person would weigh thirty-eight pounds on Mercury.

Mercury's thin atmosphere consists of trace amounts of hydrogen and helium, and the atmospheric pressure is about two trillionths of the atmospheric pressure on Earth. Since the atmosphere is so slight the sky appears pitch black except for the Sun, stars and other planets, even during the day. Mercury is the fastest moving planet in our Solar System and is thirty-six million miles from the Sun. There are no seasons on Mercury since the planet's axis is directly perpendicular to its motion. If you were on the surface of Mercury the Sun would look almost three times as big as it does from Earth! Mercury has no moons and was named after Mercury, the mythical Roman winged messenger and escort of dead souls to the underworld.

Venus

Venus is the second planet from the Sun and the hottest planet in our Solar System. Venus is covered with fast moving clouds of sulphuric acid and its thick atmosphere is mostly carbon dioxide. Its cloud cover traps the heat of the Sun, the greenhouse effect giving Venus temperatures of up to 480 degrees C. Venus has an iron core but only a very weak magnetic field. A person unprotected on the planet's surface would asphyxiate in the poisonous atmosphere, be cooked in the extreme heat and be crushed by the enormous atmospheric pressure. Venus is known as both the 'morning star' and the 'evening star' (Phosphorous and Hesperus) since it is visible and quite bright at either dawn or dusk. Venus is 7521 miles in diameter. Venus is the closest to Earth in size and mass than any of the other planets. The gravity on Venus is ninety per cent of the gravity on Earth. A 100-pound person would weigh ninety-one pounds on Venus.

The density of Venus is slightly less than the Earth's density. Venus rotates very slowly. Each day on Venus lasts 243 Earth days. A year on Venus takes 224.7 Earth days. Yes, it's true! The Venusian day is longer than its year! Venus is sixty-seven million miles from the Sun and has an almost circular orbit. Venus rotates in the opposite direction to the Earth and the other planets. Looking from the north, Venus rotates clockwise, while the other planets all rotate anti-clockwise. From Venus, the Sun would rise in the west and set in the east, the opposite of Earth. No one knows why Venus has this unusual rotation. Venus has no Moons and was named after the Roman goddess of love.

Earth

The Earth is the third planet from the Sun and is the only planet in our Solar System known to support life. The Earth is 7926 miles in diameter and is the fifth largest planet in our Solar System after Jupiter, Saturn, Uranus and Neptune. The Earth has one Moon, which may have once been a part of the Earth, having broken off during a catastrophic collision with a huge body billions of years ago. The Earth is the densest planet in the Solar System and to escape its gravitational pull an object must reach a velocity of 24 840 miles per hour.

The Earth takes 23.93 hours to rotate around its axis once. This is a sidereal day. Each year on Earth lasts 365.26 Earth days. The Earth's rotation is slowing down very slightly over time. The Earth is ninety-three million miles from the Sun. The Earth's axis is tilted from perpendicular to the plane of the ecliptic by 23 degrees 27 minutes. This tilting gives us the four seasons of the year: spring, summer, autumn and winter. Since the axis is tilted, different parts of the globe are oriented towards the Sun at different times of the year. This affects the amount of Sunlight each receives.

The Earth's atmosphere is 300 miles thick but most of the atmosphere is within ten miles of the Earth's surface. It is composed of seventy-eight per cent nitrogen, twenty-one per cent oxygen, one-tenth of a per cent argon, point zero three of one per cent carbon dioxide and trace amounts of other gases. The atmosphere was formed by planetary degassing, a process in which gases like carbon dioxide, water vapour, sulphur dioxide and nitrogen were released from the interior of the Earth from volcanoes and other processes. The temperature on Earth ranges from -88 degrees C to 58 degrees C. Life forms on Earth have modified the composition of the atmosphere since their evolution.

The Moon

The Moon is Earth's only natural satellite whose surface is studded with craters and strewn with rocks and dust. There is no atmosphere on the Moon to help protect it from bombardment by potential impactors. There is no erosion, wind or precipitation and little geological activity to wear away these craters, so the surface remains unchanged until another new impact changes it. Since sound waves travel through air, the Moon is silent because there can be no sound transmission on the Moon. Recent lunar missions indicate there might be frozen ice at the poles. The same side of the Moon always faces the Earth. The far side of the Moon was first observed in 1959 when the unmanned Soviet Luna 3 mission orbited the Moon and photographed it.

Neil Armstrong and Buzz Aldrin on NASA's Apollo 11, which included Michael Collins, were the first people to walk on the Moon on July 21st 1969. If you were standing on the Moon, the sky would always appear dark even during the daytime. From any spot on the Moon, except on the far side of the Moon where you cannot see the Earth, the Earth would always be in the same place in the sky. The Moon is in a synchronous rotation with the Earth. The phase of the Earth changes as the Earth rotates, displaying various continents.

The Moon is 238 900 miles from Earth on average. At its closest approach, its perigee, the Moon is 221 460 miles and at its farthest approach, its apogee, the Moon is 252,700 miles from the Earth. The Moon revolves around the Earth in twenty-seven days eight hours. The Moon's orbit is expanding over time as it slows down and the Earth is also slowing down as it loses energy. One billion years ago, the Moon was much closer to the Earth, less than 150 000 miles and took only twenty days to orbit the Earth. One Earth 'day' was about eighteen hours long and not twenty-four hours. The tides on Earth were much stronger since the Moon was closer. The Moon's diameter is 2140 miles and the Earth / Moon size ratio is quite large in comparison to ratios of other planet /

Moon systems. The Moon's gravitational force is only seventeen per cent of the Earth's gravity. A 100-pound person would weigh seventeen pounds on the Moon.

The temperature on the Moon ranges from daytime highs of 130 degrees C to night time lows of -110 degrees C. Many people consider the Earth and Moon to be a double planet system rather than a planet/moon system. The Moon does not actually revolve around the Earth; it revolves around the Sun in concert with the Earth like a double planet system. The sidereal and synodic lunar months have different lengths. The sidereal month is the amount of time it takes the Moon to return to the same position in the sky with respect to the stars. The sidereal month is 27.321 days long. The synodic month is the time between similar lunar phases, e.g. between two full Moons, the synodic month is 29.530 days long. When a single month has two Full Moons, the second Full Moon is called a Blue Moon.

Mars

Mars, the red planet is the fourth planet from the Sun and the most Earth-like planet in our solar system. It is half the size of Earth, has a dry rocky surface mostly covered with iron-rich dust and a very thin atmosphere. There are low-lying plains in the northern hemisphere but the southern hemisphere is dotted with impact craters. Olympus Mons, the largest volcano (now extinct) on Mars is perhaps the largest volcano in the Solar System. It is seventeen miles high and over 320 miles across. The north and south poles of Mars are covered by ice caps composed of frozen water and carbon dioxide.

Although there is no liquid water on the surface of Mars the surface shows much evidence of the effects of ancient waterways upon the landscape. There are ancient dry rivers and lakes complete with huge inflow and outflow channels. These channels were probably caused by catastrophic flooding that quickly eroded the landscape. Scientists think the water on Mars is now frozen in the land as permafrost and frozen in the polar ice caps. Mars is 4222 miles in diameter and its core is probably iron and sulphides. More will be known when data from future Mars missions arrives and is analysed. A 100-pound person would weigh thirty-eight pounds on Mars.

Each day on Mars lasts for 1.03 Earth days, 24.6 hours. A year on Mars consists of 687 Earth days. Mars is 141.6 million miles from the Sun and its orbit is quite elliptical. Mars has a thin atmosphere consisting of ninety-five per cent carbon dioxide, three per cent nitrogen, and one and half per cent argon. There is no oxygen. The atmospheric pressure is only one per cent of Earth's atmospheric pressure at sea level. Mars' surface temperature averages -63 degrees C. The temperature ranges from a high of twenty degrees C to a low of -140 degrees C. Mars has two tiny Moons, Phobos and Deimos which were probably asteroids pulled into orbit around Mars. Mars was named after the Roman god of war.

Jupiter

Jupiter is the fifth planet from the Sun and largest planet in our solar system. This gas giant has a thick atmosphere, seventeen Moons and a dark, barely visible ring. Its most prominent features are bands across its latitudes and a great red spot, which is a storm. This enormous planet radiates twice as much heat as it absorbs from the Sun and has an extremely strong magnetic field. It is slightly flattened at its poles and it bulges out a bit at the equator. Jupiter's diameter is 88 700 miles that is a little more than 11 times the diameter of the Earth. Jupiter is so big, all the other planets in our Solar System could fit inside it. Although Jupiter's mass is 318 times the mass of the Earth the gravity on Jupiter is only 254 per cent of the gravity on Earth. A 100-pound person would weigh 254 pounds on Jupiter.

It takes Jupiter nine hours fifty-five minutes to revolve around its axis and 11.86 Earth years for Jupiter to orbit the Sun once. Jupiter is made up of gases and liquids so as it rotates, its parts do not rotate at exactly the same velocity. On average, Jupiter is 480 million miles from the Sun. Jupiter has four large moons and thirteen small ones. Galileo first discovered the four largest moons Io, Europa, Ganymede and Callisto in 1610. These Moons are known as the Galilean Moons. Ganymede is the largest Moon in the Solar System.

Jupiter has faint dark rings composed of tiny rock fragments and dust. These rings were discovered by NASA's Voyager 1 in 1980. The cloud tops' average temperature is -153 degrees C. Jupiter has been known since ancient times. It is the third brightest object in the night sky after the Moon and Venus. A short period comet discovered by Eugene and Carolyn Shoemaker and David H. Levy passed close by Jupiter in 1992. Jupiter's gravitational forces broke the comet apart and it collided with Jupiter for six days during July 1994, causing huge fireballs in

Jupiter's atmosphere, visible from Earth. Jupiter was named after the Roman god, Jupiter.

Saturn

Saturn is the sixth planet from the Sun and is the second largest planet in our solar system. It has beautiful rings made mostly of ice chunks and some rocks that range in size from the size of a fingernail to the size of a car. Saturn is made mostly of hydrogen and helium gas. Saturn is visible without using a telescope, but a low power telescope is needed to see its rings. 764 Earths could fit inside Saturn. Saturn is the most oblate (flattened) planet in our Solar System. It has an equatorial diameter of 74 898 miles and a polar diameter of 67 560 miles. This is a difference of almost ten per cent. Saturn's flattened shape is caused by its fast rotation and its gaseous composition. Although Saturn's rings are extremely wide almost 185 000 miles in diameter, they are very thin, about six miles thick. The gravity on Saturn is only 1.08 times the gravity on Earth. A 100-pound person would weigh 108 pounds on Saturn.

Saturn is the only planet in our Solar System that is less dense than water. Saturn would float if there were a body of water large enough! Each day on Saturn lasts ten and one-fifth Earth days. A year on Saturn lasts 29.46 Earth years. The mean temperature on Saturn at the cloud tops is -185 degrees C. Saturn has thirty moons including the massive Titan. Saturn was named after the Roman god of agriculture.

Uranus

Uranus is the seventh planet from the Sun in our solar system. This huge, icy world is covered with clouds and is encircled by a belt of eleven rings and twenty-two Moons. Uranus' blue colour is caused by the methane (CH4) in its atmosphere; this molecule absorbs red light. Uranus' rotational axis is strongly tilted on its side 97.9 degrees. Instead of rotating with its axis roughly perpendicular to the plane of its orbit like all the other planets in our Solar System, Uranus rotates on its side along its orbital path. This tipped rotational axis gives rise to extreme seasons on Uranus. Uranus is 31 690 miles in diameter. This gas giant is the third largest planet in our Solar system. Uranus is only ninety-one per cent of the gravity on Earth. A 100-pound person would weigh ninety-one pounds on Uranus.

Each day on Uranus lasts eighteen Earth hours. A year on Uranus lasts eighty-five Earth years. Uranus is on average 1140 million miles from the Sun. The mean temperature on the surface of Uranus' cloud layer is -175 degrees C. Uranus is a frozen, gaseous planet with a molten core and its atmosphere consists of eighty-three per cent hydrogen, five per cent helium and two per cent methane. Uranus has five large moons and seventeen small moons. Uranus was discovered by the British astronomer, William Herschel on March 13th 1781. Uranus was named by the British astronomer William Herschel in 1781, after the ancient Greek god of the sky.

Neptune

Neptune is the eighth planet from the Sun in our solar system. This giant planet has a hazy atmosphere, strong winds, is orbited by eight moons and narrow, faint rings arranged in clumps. Neptune's blue colour is caused by the methane ($CH4$) in its atmosphere. Neptune cannot be seen using the eyes alone and was the first planet whose existence was predicted mathematically. Uranus's orbit was perturbed by an unknown object which turned out to be another gas giant, Neptune. The calculations were done independently by both J.C. Adams and Le Verrier. Neptune was then observed by J.G. Galle and d'Arrest on September 23, 1846. Neptune is 30 775 miles in diameter and could hold almost sixty Earths. The gravity on Neptune is only one and one-tenth times the gravity on Earth. A 100-pound person would weigh 119 pounds on Neptune.

Each day on Neptune lasts nineteen Earth hours. A year on Neptune lasts 164.8 Earth years. Since Neptune was discovered in 1846, it has just completed a single revolution around the Sun. Occasionally, Neptune's orbit is actually outside that of Pluto because Pluto has a highly eccentric (non-circular) orbit, and during this time, twenty years out of every 248 Earth years, Neptune is actually the farthest planet from the Sun and not Pluto. From January 21, 1979 until February 11, 1999, Pluto was inside the orbit of Neptune. Now, and until September 2226, Pluto is outside the orbit of Neptune. Neptune's rotational axis is tilted 30 degrees to the plane of its orbit around the Sun. This is a few degrees more than the Earth's axis and gives Neptune seasons. Each season lasts forty Earth years; the poles are in constant darkness or constant Sunlight for forty years at a time.

The mean temperature is -125 degrees C. Neptune was named after the mythical Roman god of the seas.

Pluto

Pluto is the ninth and (usually) the farthest planet from the Sun in our solar system. It is the smallest planet in our solar system and the last to be discovered. It is smaller than many of the other planets' moons, including our Moon. Pluto is 1429 miles in diameter. The gravity on Pluto is eight per cent of the gravity on Earth. A 100-pound person would weigh only eight pounds on Pluto.

Each day on Pluto lasts six and one-third Earth days. Each year on Pluto lasts 247.7 Earth years. From Pluto, the Sun looks like a tiny dot in the sky. Pluto has a very eccentric orbit and its distance from the Sun varies considerably during its orbit around the Sun. Pluto is very cold. Its average temperature is -236 degrees C. Pluto's composition is probably seventy per cent rock and thirty per cent water. This is determined from density calculations. There may be methane ice together with frozen nitrogen and carbon dioxide on the cold rocky surface. Pluto's atmosphere forms when Pluto is closest to the Sun. The solar heat vaporises frozen methane, which combines with nitrogen, a little carbon monoxide, and methane, definitely not breathable by humans. The atmospheric pressure is probably very low. When Pluto is furthest away from the Sun the methane freezes again.

Pluto has one Moon, Charon. It is small, only 700 miles in diameter. It orbits 12 000 miles from Pluto on average. It may be covered by water ice and probably has no atmosphere. Charon is in a synchronous orbit around Pluto. That is, Charon is always over the same spot on Pluto; Charon's orbit takes exactly one Pluto day. Charon was discovered in 1978 and was named after the mythological demon who ferried people across the river Styx into Hades. Pluto was named after the Roman god of the underworld, Pluto.

The Sun

Our Sun is a star located at the centre of our Solar System. It is a huge, spinning ball of hot gas and nuclear reactions that 'lights' up the Earth and provides us with heat. The Sun's absolute magnitude, its intrinsic brightness is +4.83. Its stellar type is G, a star that absorbs strong metallic lines in its spectrum. The Greeks called the Sun 'Hellos'; the Romans called it 'Sol'. The Earth is closest to the Sun around January 2nd each year, at ninety-one and a half million miles. It is farthest away from the Sun around July 2nd each year, at ninety-four and a half million miles. The Sun's core can reach fifteen million degrees C. The surface temperature is approximately 5500C. The outer atmosphere of the Sun which we can see during a total solar eclipse gets extremely hot, up to one and a half to two million degrees. At the centre of big Sunspots, the temperature can be as low as 4000 degrees C.

Its mass is seventy-five per cent hydrogen and twenty-five per cent helium. About one-tenth of a per cent is composed of metals made from hydrogen via nuclear fusion. This ratio is changing slowly over time as the nuclear reactions convert smaller atoms into more massive ones. Since the Sun formed four and a half billion years ago it has used up about half of its initial hydrogen supply. The element helium was named after the Sun 'Hellos' because it was first discovered on the Sun. Helium is plentiful on the Sun but rare on Earth. The element helium was discovered during the total solar eclipse of 1868 when a new line in the solar absorption spectrum was observed.

At the Sun's core, nuclear fusion produces enormous amounts of energy, through the process of converting hydrogen nuclei into helium nuclei, nuclear fusion. Although the nuclear output of the Sun is not entirely consistent, each second the Sun converts about 600 million tons of hydrogen nuclei into helium nuclei. These reactions convert mass (roughly four tons) into energy and release an enormous amount of heat and light energy into the Solar System. Thus the Sun loses four tons of mass each second. The Sun will run out of fuel in about five billion years. When this happens the Sun will explode into a planetary nebula, and a giant shell of gas will destroy the planets in the Solar System, including Earth.

Astronomers analyse how and why the amount of light from the Sun varies over time, the effect of the Sun's light on the Earth's climate, spectral lines, the Sun's magnetic field, the solar wind, and many other solar phenomena. Looking at the Sun can blind you or cause cataracts.

Fun Activities

Fun Activity One:
Make a Comet Nucleus

Comets are made of some of the original material from which the solar system formed. Orbiting far from the Sun, this primordial material has survived in an unaltered state for billions of years. When a comet nucleus is gravitationally drawn into the inner solar system it begins to heat up. The volatile materials from which it is made boil off to form the head and tail that have amazed, baffled and frightened people throughout history. This tremendous light show is produced from just a small, solid nucleus measuring only ten or fifteen miles long. Think of a comet as a very dirty iceberg. You can make an accurate model of a comet nucleus easily. However, it is difficult to do it tidily.

Comet Ingredients:

CAUTION: *Dry ice (even a brief exposure) will cause burns. Be careful!*

Dry Ice (two kilograms).

Water (around half a gallon) in jug.

Ammonia (a few drops or sprays of window cleaner).

Dirt, fine grained, one handful.

Worcester Sauce, a couple of drops.

Bin liners: two.

Large Bowl.

Waterproof gloves. The better insulated, the warmer your hands will remain.

Paper or Cloth Towels.

Hammer.

Mixing Spoon or Stick.

These ingredients are either actual components or analogous ones. The dry ice is frozen carbon dioxide. Water, ammonia, organic (carbon based) molecules, and silicates are all present in comet nuclei. They have been identified through spectral measurements of comet tails and the collection of tiny ice particles by very high-flying research aircraft.

Method

Line the bowl with a bin liner and place the other bin liner on the floor. Pour about a pint of water into the bowl. Add the Worcester sauce, ammonia, and some of the dirt and mix. Put on the gloves and wrap the dry ice in a cloth towel, placing it over the bin liner on the floor. Use the hammer to grind up the dry ice into a powder. Gradually pour the dry ice powder into the water, mixing as you pour. There will be lots of vapour formed. The dry ice, water and other ingredients should form a thickening slush. Keep stirring for a few seconds as it thickens. Using the bin liner to lift the slush away from the sides of the bowl, use your gloved hands to pack the slush into a ball. Keep packing and forming until the ball solidifies as a big lump. Peel back the bin liner and scatter some more dirt over the lump. Pour some of the remaining water over the lump, turning it as you do, so that a layer of water ice forms over the entire lump.

Observe the behaviour of your miniature comet nucleus. It can be handled without gloves if the water ice coating is intact. If a spot feels sticky, pour water on the spot. It hisses and pops as carbon dioxide sublimes and forces its way through weak spots in the water ice crust. On real nuclei, this results in slight jetting forces that can cause the nucleus to spin, slightly alter its orbit or split it apart. Get three or four pounds of dry ice for each nucleus you plan to make. Store it in a freezer, but place an inch-thick lining of newspaper below the dry ice to prevent cracking of the surface on which the dry ice rests.

It is fun, it is a mess, and it is one of the most memorable and scientifically accurate activities in astronomy. Wow!

Fun Activity Two:
Making Moon Craters

Impact cratering is a process found everywhere in the solar system except on the giant gaseous planets. The Earth has been heavily impacted but erosion has removed most of the craters. Perhaps the finest surviving impact crater on Earth is the Barringer Meteor Crater near Winslow, Arizona. It is three-quarters of a mile across and 650 feet deep. It was formed about 49 000 years ago when a 150 foot nickel/iron meteorite struck the desert at a speed of 25 000 miles per hour. An examination of actual craters (almost any image of the Moon will do), will prepare you for this activity. Just about all craters have deep central depressions, raised rims, and a blanket of ejected material surrounding them.

To make craters, you need a box lined with a bin liner and with sides at least four inches high; flour, three to four inches deep with at least an inch of clearance to the box rim; some dry powdered paint, red or blue; and some marbles. Place the flour in the box, packing it smoothly and firmly. Place a dusting of the paint powder over the flour. Use marbles to bombard the surface one at a time. Look for classical cratering features: basin, raised rim, ejecta blanket (visible as white flour on the coloured powder), rays, material shot out at high velocity forming lines pointing directly away from the impact site.

Keep careful records and profile drawings of the craters. Compare craters formed by different size projectiles, different velocities and different angles of impact. Different size projectiles can be dropped from measured heights so they will have common velocities. Also, remember the quality of the tests is more important than quantity. After several craters, the flour and powder paints can be mixed and re-smoothed without changing the white of the flour too much. Then a new layer of powder paint can be applied and additional experiments conducted. In real impacts, the impacting object is destroyed or broken up into small chunks. The marble will not do this and will remain whole in the crater.

Central Peak: A mountain found in the centre of large craters. It is formed by a rebound of the rock at the impact site. (The marble will be sitting there in this activity.)

Crater: A circular depression in a surface caused by an impact.

Ejecta: Material tossed out of the crater.

Ejecta Blanket: Ejecta tossed out at low speed. The material lies like a blanket around the crater.

Floor: The interior of the crater. It is flat in large craters. The marble will be there in this activity.

Rays: Ejecta tossed out of the crater at high speed. The material forms long lines pointing directly away from the crater.

Rim: The raised edge of the crater. It is formed by the outwards and upwards compression of the crater walls, not by ejecta.

Fun Activity Three:
Meteoroids and Space Debris Activity

Meteoroids and space debris present a potential hazard to astronauts and spacecraft. This activity demonstrates the penetrating power of a projectile with little mass but with high velocity.

Materials Needed:

Raw potato
Large diameter plastic straw, preferably strong plastic.

1 Hold a raw potato in one hand. While grasping the straw with the other hand, stab the potato with a quick, sharp motion. The straw should penetrate the potato and come out at the opposite end. Be careful not to strike your hand.

2 Again hold the potato and this time stab it with the straw using a slow push. The straw should bend before penetrating the potato very deeply.

Astronauts on space walks may encounter fast-moving rocky particles called meteoroids. A meteoroid can be very large with a mass of several thousand tons, or it can be very small, a micrometeoroid about the size of a grain of sand. Every day the Earth's atmosphere is struck by hundreds of thousands or even millions of meteoroids. Most never reach the surface because they are vaporised by the intense heat generated when they rub against the atmosphere. It is rare for a meteoroid to be large enough to survive the descent through the atmosphere and reach solid Earth. If it does, the meteor is called a meteorite.

In space there is no blanket of atmosphere to protect spacecraft from the full force of meteoroids. It was once believed meteoroids travelling at velocities averaging fifty miles per second would prove a great hazard to spacecraft. However, scientific satellites with meteoroid detection devices proved the hazard was minimal and that the majority of meteoroids are too small to penetrate the hull of spacecraft. Their impacts primarily cause pitting and sandblasting of the covering surface.

Of greater concern to spacecraft engineers is a relatively recent problem of spacecraft debris. Thousands of space launches have deposited many fragments of launch vehicles, paint chips, and other 'space junk' in orbit. Most particles are small, but travelling at speeds of nearly 18 000 miles per hour, they could be a significant hazard to spacecraft and to astronauts outside spacecraft on extravehicular activities.

Engineers have protected spacecraft from micrometeoroids and space junk in a number of ways, including construction of double walled shields. The outer wall constructed of foil and hydrocarbon materials that disintegrates the striking object into harmless gas that disperses on the second wall. Spacesuits provide impact protection through various fabric-layer combinations and strategically placed rigid materials. Although effective for particles of small mass, these protective strategies do little if the particle is large. It is especially important for space walking astronauts to be careful when they repair satellites or do assembly work in orbit. A lost bolt or nut could damage a future space mission through an accidental collision.

Fun Activity Four:
Harvest Corn Dollies Activity

In England, 'corn' refers to any grain, wheat, rye, or oats and good luck harvest figures called 'corn dollies' were made each year. You can make your own from corn.

Corn Husk Figure

Material needed: Corn husks, fresh or dried, about six to eight pieces; string; about four cotton wools balls; scraps of cloth; yarn; beads and pipe cleaners. If you are using dried husks, soak them in water to soften them. Fresh husks need no special preparation.

i. Take a strip of husk and place a few cotton balls in the middle, twisting and tying it with string to make a head. Make some arms by folding another husk and tying it near each end to make hands. Slip the arms between the husks that extend under the head. Tie the waist with string.

ii Arrange enough husks around the figure's waist so they overlap slightly. Tie them in place with string.

iii Fold the husks down carefully. For a woman wearing a long skirt, cut the husks straight across at the hem. To make a man divide the skirt in two and tie each half at the ankles. Let the figure dry completely.

You can use wallpaper remnants to practise. Cut the wallpaper into half-inch strips of about three to six feet in length.

Harvest Knot

Corn dollies have deep pagan symbolic roots and straw plaiting has a direct connection to the Celtic Spirit. The harvest knot for men has no seeds but the woman's knot has the seeds intact. It is about fertility and the wondrous bounty of the harvest. Perhaps the best-known corn sculpture is the 'cailleach', which is constructed from the last sheaf to be harvested. It is blessed and carried by the lucky person who harvested it, to give him / her good luck. Much of the pagan meanings have been forgotten. The designs and the activity of plaiting persist and today harvest knots can be made into beautiful gifts for friends. Plaiting begins with a simple pattern known as the two plait. From completed two plaits one can braid ever more complex harvest knots and corn dollies. With a little practice, one can move on to complex plaits and designs.

You may find it difficult to find straw. If you find yourself in a wheat field the best straw for plaiting should be a longer variety. You should cut the straw when almost ripe but not totally dry, the first joint still green. If the heads are bent, the straw will be too brittle. The straw should be dried in the Sun for a day and hung in bundles from a rafter upside down. When straw is dry, take off the outer leaf and cut the head off at the first node beneath it. Select straws similar in size to be worked together. Try it and enjoy your encounter with the ancient rhythms of Celtic antiquity.

Tables

Meteor Showers

Shower	Peak	Detectable-Dates	Meteors per hour
Quadrantids	Jan-3	Jan-1-4	40
Lyrids	Apr-21	Apr-19-24	5
Eta-Aquarids	May-4	Apr-21-May-12	20
Delta-Aquarids	July-29	July-15-Aug-18	10
Perseids	Aug-12	July-25-Aug-17	50
Orionids	Oct-21	Oct-18-19	20
Taurids	Nov-1	Oct-15-Dec-1	5
Leonids	Nov-16	Nov-14-20	5
Geminids	Dec-13	Dec-7-15	50
Ursids	Dec-22	Dec-17-24	15

Origin of the Names of the Days of the Week

Sunday: The name comes from the Latin dies solis, meaning 'sun's day': the name of a pagan Roman holiday.

Monday: The name comes from the Anglo-Saxon monandaeg, the 'moon's day'. This second day was sacred to the goddess of the moon.

Tuesday: This day was named after the Norse god Tyr. The Romans named this day after their war-god Mars: dies Martis and in Sweden tisdag.

Wednesday: The day named to honour Wodan (Odin). The Romans called it dies Mercurii, after their god Mercury.

Thursday: The day named after the Norse god Thor. In the Norse languages this day is called Torsdag. The Romans named this day dies Jovis 'Jove's Day', after Jove or Jupiter, their most important god.

Friday: The day in honour of the Norse goddess Frigg. In Old High German this day was called frigedag. To the Romans this day was sacred to the goddess Venus.

Saturday: This day was called dies Saturni, 'Saturn's Day', by the ancient Romans in honour of Saturn. In Anglo-Saxon: sater daeg.

Origin of the Names of the Months of the Year

January: Janus, Roman god of doors, beginnings, sunset and sunrise, had one face looking forward and one backward.

February: On February 15th the Romans celebrated the festival of forgiveness of sins. Februare: Latin to purify.

March: Mars, the Roman god of war.

April: Roman month Aprilis, derived from aperire, Latin to open, as in opening buds and blossoms, and from Aphrodite, original Greek name of Venus.

May: Maia, Roman goddess, mother of Mercury by Jupiter, and daughter of Atlas.

June: Juno, chief Roman goddess.

July: Renamed for Julius Caesar in 44 BC, who was born this month; Quintilis, Latin for fifth month, was the former name. The Roman year began in March rather than January.

August: Formerly Sextilis, sixth month in the Roman calendar. Re-named in 8 BC for Augustus Caesar.

September: September, septem, Latin for seven, the seventh month in the Julian or Roman calendar, established in the reign of Julius Caesar.

October: Eighth month, octo, Latin for eight in the Julian, Roman calendar. The Gregorian calendar instituted by Pope Gregory XIII established January as the first month of the year.

November: Ninth Roman month. Novem, Latin for nine. Catholic countries adopted the Gregorian calendar in 1582, skipping ten days that October, correcting for too many leap years.

December: Julian, Roman year's tenth month. Decem, Latin for ten.

The Evening Sky

Walter Berg produces a monthly astro update, highlighting interesting celestial events and their Earthly connections.

How to get The Evening Sky Via the World Wide Web

Each bulletin is uploaded to the World Wide Web every month, so simply bookmark the following link and check it out on the first of every month!

http://www.theeveningsky.co.uk

How to get The Evening Sky Via Email

Send an email to: subscribe@theeveningsky.co.uk

How to get The Evening Sky Via the Amateur Radio Packet Network

If you are a licensed radio amateur and are connected to the Packet Radio Network send a message with your full packet radio address to:

2E1GJN@GB7BEN.#43.GBR.EU. You will be added to the distribution list and early every month you should receive your personal copy at your local BBS.

The Evening Sky web site, and email service are designed and maintained by

Paul Rudkin of Winslow, Buckinghamshire. U.K. Paul has run The Evening Sky web site since 1995 and continues to enhance it on a regular basis. Paul studied Electrical and Electronic Engineering at De Montfort University and now works as a senior software engineer for a leading supplier and integrator of assembly, test and material handling equipment that is sold worldwide. Paul may be found on the web at

http://www.thegithouse.com—email: paul@thegithouse.com

How to get The Evening Sky by Mail

To subscribe to The Evening Sky astro news-sheet write to uvshift, PO Box 5212, Central Milton Keynes, MK9 3HD, UK. Or you can contact Walter Berg by email:

walterberg@theeveningsky.co.uk

The Phenomenon Research Association

The Phenomenon Research Association (PRA) originally formed in 1991 to investigate UFO sightings around the Derbyshire area, England. The PRA currently investigate UFO sightings across the world and have a large membership including: business consultants, authors, nuclear engineers, Post Office engineers and enlightened members of the public.

The PRA is one of many independent organisations formed to investigate and study UFO phenomena. Since the PRA began their activities, their investigations and reports have been widely recognised for their high quality resulting in links with France, Belgium, Germany, Spain, Guatemala and Australia. There is a close liaison between many UFO investigation groups leading to a free exchange of information on existing UFO activity.

Camcorder technology has increased the video footage available for viewing UFO objects and craft of various types. Video evidence together with witness interrogation forms are a valuable tool in the study of this subject. The PRA specialise in one type of UFO: the mysterious Flying Triangle Craft (FT). Information gained from witness interviews is forwarded on a daily basis to the Project's database held in Berlin. With a number of European UFO groups involved in this undertaking the project has gained some international significance. The subsequent analysis of UFO events has enabled researchers to follow the course of a Flying Triangle across England on a number of occasions. There is particular concern over their disturbing interest in Nuclear Power Stations.

Omar Fowler, leader of The Phenomenon Research Association is a regular contributor to television and radio and has published widely. He is a Director: Flying Saucer Review and a consultant: 'Mu' Magazine Japan. His booklets: Crop Circles: The Final Solution and The Flying Triangle Mystery were particularly insightful and successful.

The Phenomenon Research Association produces a bi-monthly magazine: OVNI priced £1.00; and hold regular meetings and discussion groups addressed by internationally known experts in the field.

If you are interested in UFO phenomena or related activities you may contact The Phenomenon Research Association by email: bontor@raol.com.

Horoscopes

To receive information or to order a horoscope please email

horoscopes@uvshift.com

or write to Horoscopes, uvshift, PO Box 5212, Central Milton Keynes, MK9 3HD. All uvshift need from you, are: the place, the date and the time of your birth.

Sole Agent for Boris Heiman: Traditional Western Horoscopes—Traditional Western astrology, the one you are probably most familiar with uses the tropical zodiac.

Sole Agent for Naseem Ghosh: Nirayana or Indian Vedic Horoscopes—Nirayana or Vedic astrology uses the sidereal movable zodiac.

Sole Agent for David Goldstein: New Zodiac Constellational Horoscopes—New Zodiac astrology uses the constellational, sidereal movable zodiac.

Your Horoscope: Each horoscope is a unique booklet crafted specifically for you and you alone. Computers calculate the precise positions of the planets and the interpretation is written and approved by our International Consultant Astrologers.

What can a Horoscope do?

The purpose of Astrology is not to foretell but to reveal. Through your Birth Chart you will come to understand clearly your own unique place in the cosmos, thereby, understanding yourself, your relationships and your aspirations.

A—Character Portrait

A Character Portrait is a full interpretation of your Birth Chart. It highlights personality traits and hidden talents and indicates your career options and route to successful relationships. A4, 30 page booklet: £22

B—Marriage & Compatibility Profile

A Compatibility (Synastry) Profile is a detailed document comparing two charts. This comparison helps you to make the most of your relationship. Besides the central theme of love, the Compatibility Chart also covers mental rapport, sexual attraction and the stability of the relationship. A4, 30 page booklet: £22

C—Yearly Forecast

A Forecast is not a prediction but an in-depth look at what is happening to you now and the influences over the next twelve months. By following the patterns, rhythms, circles and cycles of the planets and the phases of the Moon it enables you to plan for moods and energy cycles. A Forecast helps you to know when you are in top form and when you will be at your most efficient. A4, 30 page booklet: £22

D—Combination of Character Profile and Yearly Forecast

A Combination of CP + YF offers your Birth Chart, aspects, character and general life trends combined with your Transit Chart, aspects, month by month trends and general analysis. A4, 40 page booklet: £35

Horoscopes printed in Japanese are available from: NSC, 101 Hazawa Court, 3-17-7 Hirro, Shibuya-ku, Tokyo, Japan T150. Prices quoted individually.

The New Zodiac

Zodiac Astrology: Relationship, Love and Sex
David Goldstein

Publication date: October 2002   Pages: 164

ISBN 0-9540211-1-8   Paperback

Price £7.95   Size 198 mm x 128 mm

In our love and sexual relationships we interact with each other on many energy levels and if we fail to understand the energies involved, misunderstanding, heartache, dissatisfaction and tension can occur.

New Zodiac Astrology: Relationships, Love and Sex explores all aspects of the new zodiac and sun sign compatibility. New zodiac astrology will help you to generate positive energy in your love relationships, understand each other better in your day-to-day life and gain satisfaction and pleasure in your sexual union.

New zodiac astrology tells you exactly what to do immediately to improve your relationships in the areas of life, love and sex. Your most compatible new zodiac astrology partner will be very different from the partner advised by traditional astrology.

Two self-assessment forms at the end of the book will enable you to see yourself as your partner sees you. Your Libido Scale explores your sex drive and sexual preference. The Relationship Quiz tells you how well you know your partner. Both are great fun to complete and can be completed by your partner too. Indeed, the Relationship Quiz requires your partner's participation.

We all enjoy reading our horoscope, yet we know the traditional signs of the zodiac are hopelessly out of date. The ancient civilisations of Mesopotamia founded astrology and passed their knowledge to the Greeks and Romans. The Greeks and Romans personalised astrology and arranged astrology into the format we know today.

2500 years ago the sun entered the sign of the zodiac Aries on March 21. Today the sun no longer enters Aries on March 21. Today the sun is moving through the zodiac sign of Pisces on March 21. All of the original signs of the zodiac have been displaced and new signs have entered the zodiac.

The amount of time the sun spends in each zodiac sign has also changed. The sun actually spends forty-five days in Virgo and only six days in Scorpio. The sign of Ophiuchus, the Healer (November 29 to December 16) has moved between the zodiac signs of Scorpio and Sagittarius. On March 27 the sun partially touches the sign of Cetus. Two further signs: Orion and Sextans lie within the zodiac but the sun does not touch these two signs. Remember the zodiac is the band of sky at each side of the sun so it is possible for a sign to be in the zodiac and yet not be a sun sign.

David Goldstein is an internationally known Astrologer based in London and Tokyo. David Goldstein has produced horoscopes and offered advice to US, UK and Japanese celebrities and politicians.

Blood Type: Preference, Behaviour and Personality
H.S. Hisami

Publication date: October 2002   Pages: 164

ISBN 0-9540211-2-6178 Paperback

Price £7.95 Size 198 mm x 128 mm

Blood Type: Preference, Behaviour and Personality offers another key to unlocking the door to biological patterns, which underlie behaviour. Your blood type controls your emotional responses to stress and shapes the way you perceive the world. Blood Type: Preference, Behaviour and Personality provides a map and builds another layer of consciousness by which we can understand others and ourselves in a positive way, and appreciate the differences between us.

Type O is the basic human blood Type and over 50,000 years old, Type A appeared around 20,000 years ago, Type B appeared about 10,000 years ago and Type AB is very recent, appearing around 1,000 years ago and still makes up only 4% of the population.

The emergence of new blood Types arose as a necessity to adapt to different environmental conditions, which required different lifestyles thus producing different behavioural patterns and different thinking, patterns which optimised survival opportunities.

Type O	Capable of destroying anyone: friend or foe
Type A	Cooperative personality designed to get along in crowded environments
Type B	Balance between the tensions of the mind and the physical demands of the body
Type AB	Merger of the tolerant Type A and the formerly barbaric but more balanced Type B

Hisami is one of Japan's leading blood type and personality specialists. He has spent seven years studying western blood type including UK populations. Blood Type: Preference, Behaviour and Personality explains in simple terms how different blood types are interested in different things, are drawn to different fields and often find it hard to understand other blood types.

The Sagittarius Network
Neil Green

Publication date: March 2003   Pages: 178

ISBN 0-9540211-3-4 Paperback

Price £7.95 Size 198 mm x 128 mm

An alien civilisation far more advanced than our own has influenced life on Earth, without detection for thousands of years. Their secret messages have now been detected but not completely deciphered.

Our science has barely begun to understand the deeper physics of the cosmos but new evidence indicates the Sagittarius Network is part of a cosmic spiders web continually vibrating the fabric of space/time and whose influence spans our entire cosmic domain.

Who really taught the Egyptians to build pyramids and how were an unknown illiterate tribe able to construct Stonehenge? How could ancient cultures know about the existence of star ships? Where did the catalyst responsible for the advancement of astronomy, mathematics, science and philosophy really come from? Neil Green unravels the truth, revealing an alien intelligence not only influenced events on Earth and in our solar system but controlled events throughout our galaxy.

Apollo astronauts left many scientific experiments behind on the surface of the Moon. The US space administration, NASA, and the 'dark-siders' (the world military-intelligence community and powerful secret societies who not only work to dubious ends but are privy to occult powers) have been collecting data from those experiments for the past thirty years. German scientists have interpreted information from one lunar experiment, laser-ranging equipment, with startling results. There has been no cover up—yet there is a code of silence.

A region of space within the star constellation of Sagittarius is generating enormous energy fields. Hidden within the deepest layers of space-time are signals, which instantaneously travel 30 000 light-years across the galaxy and influence life on Earth. These signals are our messages from the gods.

In his fascinating book Neil Green uncovers the secrets of The Sagittarius Network and exposes the 'dark-siders' ' struggle to control knowledge and liberty.

The UFO Handbook
Samuel B. Davis

   Publication date: October 2003 Pages 178

   ISBN 0-9540211-4-2 Paperback

   Price £9.95 Size 198 mm x 128 mm

This is the definitive UFO compendium examining every aspect of UFOology from first sighting to latest alien abduction.

All governments of the world deny the existence of UFOs. Yet all governments produce disaster-training manuals, which include sections entitled 'Alien Attack and UFO Potential'. UFOs are taken very seriously by the military and by government intelligence gathering organisations.

The UFO Handbook explains, lists, categorises and reveals everything you need to know:

UFO Classification System	UFOs: Regional Power Blackouts
UFO Shapes	UFOs: The Panic Hazard
UFO Sightings	UFOs: Emergency Action
UFO Secrecy	UFOs: Inside the Military
UFO Adverse Potential	UFOs: Underground
UFO Hazards	UFOs: NATO and the CIA
UFO Abduction	UFOs: Propulsion Systems

The UFO Handbook is not only a revelation to read but an invaluable source of reference for every UFO lay person, enthusiast or member of the fraternity.

The Golden Book of Omikuji
Y. Watanabe

Publication date: June 2003 Pages 100
ISBN 0-9540211-5-0 Paperback
Price £6.95 Size 198 mm x 128 mm

Omikuji is the ancient Japanese craft of fortune telling practised at shrines or temples since before the Edo period.

A lucky stick on which a number is written is selected at random from many sticks standing in a large tube. A shrine maiden takes your lucky stick and matches the number on it to a written oracle, a piece of paper on which your fortune is written.

General fortune from excellent luck to bad luck is written in Omikuji and individual fortune such as love, relationships, marriage, health, money, illness, journey, business transactions, entrance exams, lost articles and so forth are predicted.

The Golden Book of Omikuji explores the history and magic of this art. Your fortune for each day will be told. You select a golden Omikuji number and you rather than the shrine maiden look up the corresponding oracle to find your fortune.

Seven categories of fortune are predicted
- Great luck
- Better luck   Bad luck
- Good luck   Worst luck
- Small luck   Ill fate

Y. Watanabe has been practising Omikuji for many years and is recognised as a virtuoso of this ancient golden art.

All of our books are available through your local bookseller, or you can order direct from uvshift, please contact:

uvshift, ~~~~~~~~~~~~~~~~~~~~~~ lton Keynes, MK9 3HD.
e-mail: ~~~~~~~~~~~~~~~~~~~~~~ www.uvshift.com

Karl Parkinson
Uvshift - First Floor
69 Tottenham Court Road
London W1T 2HA

ALL ORDERS ARE POSTAGE FREE (in the UK)

Walter Berg has published over a dozen books. Below are his best selling titles:

> *The Signs of the Zodiac* (Harper/Collins) 1994
> *The Bergian System of Astrology* (Shodensha) 1995
> *The Second Bergian System of Astrology* (Fu-So-Sha) 1996
> *The Bergian System of Relationship Astrology* (Fu-So-Sha) 1997
> *Voice of the Heavens* (Fu-So-Sha) 1998 (Hardback)
> *Your Brilliant Guide to the 1999 Total Solar Eclipse* (Sigma Press) 1999
> *The Bergian System of Astrology & Blood Type* (Fushaso) 2000

Walter Berg writes a weekly astrology column in the national Japanese newspaper, San Kei (circulation: five million). He has written over one thousand articles for leading Japanese and UK newspapers and magazines including: Domani, Junie and Esse.

Walter Berg's 'Bergian Astrology Corner' was broadcast each Monday afternoon on the 'Big Today' programme, Fuji Television between April and August 1996. (Big Today is networked nationally with an audience of eleven million.) Walter Berg still appears on Fuji Television via NTV News

Walter broadcasts each month on local BBC and independent radio stations and occasionally on national radio. He has contributed to several television magazine programmes and news items.

Walter produces horoscopes and psychological profiles and has constructed astrological profiles for many Japanese celebrities, film stars and politicians; including Madam Doi, Leader of the House and Mr. Tanaka, former Secretary to the Prime Minister. He is the world's leading authority on the science of Constellational Astrology and also a leading expert in other astrological systems: Western Tropical, Eastern Sidereal, Meng, Celtic, etc.

Representation

UK	UK/Japanese Link	Japan
uvshift	LOE Entertainments 159 Broadhurst Gardens London UK NW6 3AU	NSC 101 Hazawa Court 3-17-7 Hiroo-Shibuya Tokyo Japan T150

Karl Parkinson
Uvshift - First Floor
69 Tottenham Court Road
London W1T 2HA

nearly £200, which I happily transferred into the Thai bank account.

Sadly, the landlords have retired to France after twenty-four years of running it, so it has now been sold. It will be continuing as before initially, so all the patrons are thrilled to know that the legendary quiz nights are going to be maintained to principally raise more money for local charities.

When this book is eventually published, I will also be earmarking some of the profits for the DRCS, which, in November 2011, became officially registered as the Dog and Cat Rescue Samui Foundation. They are now keeping successfully afloat since travel restrictions were lifted after the pandemic, and tourists are increasingly returning to Thailand again. I doubt if I will ever go back, though, as advancing age does have its limitations, especially on long-haul flights. Increased insurance also makes it financially more difficult. In the 'Thailand' period between 1998 and 2011, it seemed far less difficult to fly around the world and much easier when age is on your side! They were my golden years, but I do still take holidays abroad, though much nearer to home, like Greece, Spain, France, and Croatia.

One of the particularly long walks we took with our dogs was along the canal that runs through Bollington, parallel to the Middlewood Way, to a very small village called Whitely Green. It is a very idyllic journey, as you can imagine, and we often conversed with the many barge owners and dog walkers on the way. It always resulted in us spending an hour or two in the Windmill Pub and Restaurant. Dogs were very welcome in the fields with bar areas designated for 'families only', 'adults only', and, of course, inside the building itself. On the way back, a visit to the Cafe Waterside was always essential for coffee and homemade scones.

Having no dogs at all now, when I occasionally decide to take this walk on my own, it can be quite emotional. Most of the passing walkers have their dogs with them, and I have gradually made friends with some of them, plus some barge owners. None of those could possibly own dogs that have had the intricate adventures that Gypsy experienced, that's for sure!

On August 15th, 2021, I received a very upsetting email informing me that Brigitte had passed away from cancer after a long illness. I was so upset, as we had known her for 22 years, just prior to meeting Gypsy. What a remarkable woman she was, being a saviour to the dog and cat population. Unflinchingly, she gave her life to animal welfare despite all the odds being against her so many times.

Many TV companies around the world visited the DRCS over a period of time, and some of their films can be viewed on YouTube. In 1966 a wonderful film was produced based on Elsa the Lioness, which starred Virginia McKenna and Bill Travers. Some enterprising film company should immortalise Brigitte in a similar way in a biopic, as she deserves worldwide recognition for all she did. Regrettably, I am sure this will never happen.

Marcus

Thailand

Account Name: Dog and Cat Rescue Samui Foundation
Account holder: Dog and Cat Rescue Samui Foundation
Bank: Siam Commercial Bank
Branch: Chaweng 2 Branch
28/7 Moo 3, Bophut, Koh Samui, Suratthani 84320 Thailand
Branch code:
Account number: 836-207183-4
SWIFT code: SICOTHBK

United Kingdom

Name: Dog and Cat Rescue Samui
Camille Andrews & Marina Andrews
3 Combe View
Hungerford
Berkshire
RG17 0BZ
Phone: +44(0)1488 684538

E-mail: dogandcatrescuesamui@yahoo.co.uk